Prime Time 7/8

Language in Use

Georg Hellmayr
Stephan Waba

www.oebv.at

Overview: Test formats

Exercise		MC	BGF	OGF	ED	WF
Unit 1:	8/7	×				
Unit 2:	11/5		×			
	13/10			×		
Unit 3:	17/5		×			
	18/6a		×			
Unit 4:	20/2	×				
Unit 5:	25/2	×				
	28/6				×	
Unit 6:	30/3	×				
	31/4					×
	32/5		×			
	33/7					×
Unit 7:	35/2					×
	38/5					×
Unit 8:	40/3	×				
	42/4					×
	43/5	×				
Unit 9:	47/3			×		
Unit 10:	52/4				×	
	52/5				×	
	53/6	×				
Unit 11:	54/2			×		
	57/5	×				
	58/6		×			
Unit 12:	60/2a	×				
Unit 13:	66/3		×			
	67/6				×	

Exercise		MC	BGF	OGF	ED	WF
Unit 14:	71/2c					×
	73/4a				×	
Unit 15:	76/3	×				
	78/5				×	
Unit 16:	81/3		×			
Unit 17:	84/2				×	
	86/4					×
	87/5	×				
	88/6a		×			
Unit 18:	90/2	×				
	91/3b				×	
Unit 19:	95/3	×				
	96/4a		×			
	97/5					×
	98/6				×	
Unit 20:	100/2c			×		
	103/4a				×	
SMT:	104/1	×				
	105/2		×			
	106/3			×		
	106/4				×	
	107/5					×
	108/6	×				
	109/7		×			
	110/8			×		
	111/9				×	
	112/10					×

Units 1 to 10: Prime Time 7 (ISBN 978-3-209-07160-6 | SBNR 155138)
Units 11 to 20: Prime Time 8 (ISBN 978-3-209-07161-3 | SBNR 160179)

MC = Multiple choice | **BGF** = Banked gap fill | **OGF** = Open gap fill | **ED** = Editing | **WF** = Word formation
SMT = Sample Matura tasks

Table of contents

You will need internet access to complete this task.

This type of excercise introduces the formats of the *Standardisierte Reifeprüfung* and other standardised tests.

Prime Time 7

The British today

1 Describing places, describing people

a) Which of the words below can you use to describe places, which can you use to describe people, and which are suitable for both? Write the words into the appropriate columns.

adorable • affluent • agricultural • ancient • attractive • barren • bleak • brave •
busy • cheerful • clean • confident • cosmopolitan • crowded • cruel • cultural •
deforested • depopulated • determined • developing • dirty • dry • dynamic •
energetic • fertile • filthy • flat • formal • frank • generous • gifted • glamorous •
handsome • hard-working • hospitable • humid • humorous • industrial • jolly •
kind-hearted • lively • lovely • low-lying • lush • magnificent • modern • monotonous •
mountainous • mysterious • nearby • nervous • outgoing • overcrowded • peaceful •
perfect • picturesque • plain • pleasing • polite • polluted • punctual • quiet •
reserved • respectful • romantic • rough • rude • run-down • rural • self-assured •
selfish • slow-paced • sociable • splendid • steep • thoughtful • timid • tolerant •
traditional • tropical • unbiased • unspoilt • urban • varied • wild • worried

Words to describe places	Words to describe people	Words suitable for both
	adorable	

b) In the list of words above, there are a number of opposites. Complete the chart with the appropriate opposites.

Word	Opposite
1. agricultural	urban
2. clean	
3. crowded	
4. fertile	
5. flat	

Word	Opposite
6. humid	
7. modern	
8. run-down	
9. timid	
10. varied	

2 Land for sale

Complete the advertisement below with suitable words from task 1a.

Green Street Farmhouse is a ....lovely.... **(1)** detached farmhouse surrounded by .... **(2)** gardens featuring .... **(3)** views over the surrounding countryside and beyond.

Being located within the .... **(4)** village of Harvington, just outside Evesham, provides ideal access to the village's local facilities together with more extensive shopping facilities available in the

.... **(5)** market towns of Evesham and Stratford.

The red brick farmhouse provides generously proportioned accommodation throughout. It is surrounded by a .... **(6)** plot of garden. A raised patio provides a sunny seating area and access through to the house. There are .... **(7)** open front barns with ideal future potential for further development.

3 Portraying the British, portraying yourself

a) Complete the text below with suitable words from task 1a.

Every culture has its own social and .....cultural..... **(1)** codes, and the UK is no exception.

British people are generally known for their good manners and for being .... **(2)**. Queuing, or standing in line, is very common in the UK. Jumping a queue is considered to be very .... **(3)**. Many British people appear modest and .... **(4)**, which can show through sometimes in an unwillingness to complain about something directly.

In academic and business life, being .... **(5)** is especially important. You should always be on time for classes, lectures and meetings with academic and administrative staff.

British people are .... **(6)**, but their sense of humour is traditionally based on sarcasm and irony, which can make it difficult to understand whether someone is joking or being serious. This may take some time to get used to.

b) Use as many words from task 1a as possible to write a text comparing stereotypes for people from Britain and from your country.

4 Prepositions: Scottish independence

Complete the following text with suitable prepositions.

Around a third ....*of*........ **(1)** Scotland's four million voters believe that Scotland should leave the UK and become independent, ending the 305-year-old political union .... **(2)** England. They believe Scotland would flourish if it had much greater autonomy. A majority of Scots disagree. They believe Scotland is more secure .... **(3)** the UK, but many want the Scottish parliament to have greater financial and legal powers.

The complex and often turbulent relationship .... **(4)** the two neighbours goes back .... **(5)** Roman times, when the Roman emperor Hadrian built a wall .... **(6)** the northern end of Britain to keep .... **(7)** the marauding Scottish tribes. Yet, it turned out that the Scots more often had to fight off attempts .... **(8)** their larger neighbour attacking Scotland, rather than the other way round.

In 1613, King James VI .... **(9)** Scotland also became king of England, but the parliamentary union wasn't actually secured .... **(10)** ninety-four years later. Scottish acceptance of the 1707 Act of Union was the result .... **(11)** a combination of factors, including an economic crisis which had ruined the country financially. The Scottish Parliament was abolished .... **(12)** return .... **(13)** forty-five seats in the House of Commons .... **(14)** Westminster. The Scots began to pay English taxes, but retained their own legal and educational systems as well as their churches. Resentment simmered, but the two serious challenges to the Union in 1715 and 1745 both failed.

In the nineteenth century, the Scots played a significant role .... **(15)** the emergence of imperial Britain as soldiers, colonisers and traders. But Scottish nationalism was always present, just .... **(16)** the surface of daily life, as the Scots continued to campaign .... **(17)** some form of "home rule". In 1998, Edinburgh got a regional government.. **(18)** wide-ranging powers over education, justice and health policies, but with the UK government in charge .... **(19)** most taxation, social welfare and the economy, plus defence and foreign policy issues.

(Roland Flamini, *World Affairs Journal*, May/June 2013; adapted and abridged)

5 Reflexive and reciprocal pronouns: Royal babies

Read the following text and put the correct reflexive or reciprocal pronoun into each of the gaps. Leave the gap empty if no pronoun is required.

Prince William is issuing charming information about his son, is amusing ......*himself*...... **(1)** with his young family, obviously feeling .... **(2)** delighted in Prince George's every action. Thus we hear that young George is "at his most vocal" at 3 a.m. Prince William and the Duchess of Cambridge obviously love .... **(3)**. To an extent unseen before, this royal baby – and his parents – have been exposed to the public gaze.

 Traditionally, the arrival of royal babies met with political involvement from the start, with the Home Secretary required to be present at the birth. Yet, it has changed .... **(4)** a great deal over the years. In 1840, before Queen Victoria gave birth to her first child, the cabinet, the archbishop of Canterbury, the bishop of London and the Lord Steward gathered outside the royal bedchamber. The door was open and the Lord Steward could see and hear .... **(5)** all that went on. Moments after her birth, the infant Princess Victoria was carried naked into the outer room and laid on a prepared table to be inspected .... **(6)** by the councillors.

When the Queen and Princess Margaret were born, Home Secretaries were on the premises but George VI, wisely, terminated this practice before the birth of Prince Charles. Today, royal babies are born in hospitals, so their first public showing comes a day after their birth, when they are carried out .... **(7)** into the glare of the media, in their mother's arms – witness Prince William in 1982, and Prince George in 2013. Though the media has become more cynical and less respectful, they remain hungry for stories about the infant prince.

6 Infinitive or gerund: What defines Britishness?

Read the following text. Then decide whether the verbs from the box should be used as a gerund or an infinitive (with or without **to***) to fill the gaps.*

> ask • be (2x) • ~~define~~ • feel • include • lead • say

The monarchy, the BBC and pubs are among the most important aspects when it comes to ....*defining*........ **(1)** Britain, according to a new study. However, the pride of Britons in their national identity has fallen to an all-time low, with only one in five young people .... **(2)** they are "very proud" to be British, the British Social Attitudes survey has found.

According to the figures, shown in *The Sunday Times*, a third of people claimed .... **(3)** very proud to be British, compared with 43% a decade ago. The young and highly educated are the least likely to be .... **(4)** proud of being British, when compared to older people or those with fewer qualifications. Penny Young of NatCen Social Research, which carried out the survey, attributed the drop to factors .... **(5)** the fallout from the war in Iraq and the faltering economy. "There was a lot of confidence in Britain in 2003, but now we are still recovering from the financial crash," she said. "For some people, greater exposure to other countries through budget travel and a wider digital community can .... **(6)** them .... **(7)** what it means to be British."

Proud or not, almost three quarters of people **(74%)** see Britain as .... **(8)** defined by the monarchy. While 73% see William Shakespeare as the most important figure when it comes to defining Britishness, 73% also chose the common law system and the House of Commons. The British Social Attitudes survey has been conducted every year since 1983. The 2013 study consisted of interviews with 3,244 people, of whom 900 were asked about their level of pride in Britain.

(Alice Philipson, *The Telegraph*, 13 April 2014; adapted and abridged)

7 Language in use: Why Britain should stay in the EU

You are going to read a text about Great Britain's relationship to the European Union. Some words are missing from the text. Choose the correct answer (A, B, C or D) for each gap (1–10) in the text. Write your answers in the boxes provided. The first one (0) has been done for you.

Should Britain … **(0)** the European Union? Or should it stay? What, indeed, would quitting mean? A current book comes to the … **(Q1)** that Britain's existing EU membership is valuable, there is a great chance to make it better, and all the … **(Q2)** are worse.

It would be a historic error to pull out, author Hugo Dixon states in his new book *The In/Out Question*. Britain's economy would … **(Q3)** if it quit and its global influence would also be diminished. The UK now accounts for less than one per cent of the world's population and less than three per cent of global income (GDP). Britain will find it increasingly hard to get its voice heard on topics that … **(Q4)** its prosperity and well-being if it leaves the EU.

Dixon openly compares the problems of the EU with its chances and opportunities. On the one hand, he criticises that the EU often … **(Q5)** with things that are best left to nation states; that the European Parliament seems like a travelling circus, shuttling back and forth between Brussels and Strasbourg; and that EU … **(Q6)** are sometimes difficult for the member states to deal with.

On the other hand, he points out what is good within the EU. Most importantly, the single market gives British business … **(Q7)** to the entire EU with its 500 million consumers. Furthermore, when British companies negotiate with America, China or Japan, they are doing so as part of the world's largest trade bloc, which … **(Q8)** for nearly 20 per cent of the world's GDP. If Britain were on its own, the balance of power would be quite different.

The single market is based on what are known as the "four freedoms": the free movement of goods, services, capital and people. In Britain, the free movement of people is the … **(Q9)** of heated debate. Indeed, a desire to keep foreigners out of Britain is the main reason why the electorate may want to quit the EU entirely.

Immigration is undoubtedly an emotive topic. But allowing free movement of people within the EU has been good for Britain's economy, Dixon argues. It has also … **(Q10)** their culture and given their own citizens more opportunities to work, study and retire across the Channel. If Britain left the EU, it is not at all clear what would happen to these citizens.

(Hugo Dixon, *The Independent*, 25 March 2014; adapted and abridged)

0	A	end	B	get off	C	quit	D	live
Q1	A	idea	B	conclusion	C	information	D	result
Q2	A	elections	B	compromises	C	alternatives	D	substitutes
Q3	A	grieve	B	hurt	C	suffer	D	ache
Q4	A	affect	B	effect	C	react	D	change
Q5	A	influences	B	meddles	C	inflates	D	mixes
Q6	A	assignments	B	authorities	C	controls	D	regulations
Q7	A	access	B	excess	C	acceptance	D	balance
Q8	A	accounts	B	counts	C	is responsible	D	includes
Q9	A	episode	B	incident	C	task	D	subject
Q10	A	sacrificed	B	educated	C	enriched	D	reduced

0	Q1	Q2	Q3	Q4	Q5	Q6	Q7	Q8	Q9	Q10
C ✓										

Health issues

1 Finding the right meaning

Match the words on the left with the correct definitions or examples on the right.

1. allergy	I	**A**	throbbing headache
2. mineral supplements		**B**	adding salt, herbs and spices to food
3. addictive		**C**	extremely overweight
4. ingredients		**D**	illness
5. obese		**E**	substance to make up for sth. lacking in a person's diet
6. disease		**F**	sth. to drink
7. saliva		**G**	causing sb. to become dependent on e.g. a substance
8. seasoning		**H**	food substances needed to prepare a certain dish
9. migraine		**I**	negative physical reaction to a substance (esp. food)
10. beverage		**J**	watery liquid in your mouth

2 Prepositional phrases 1: Matching

Write the correct prepositional phrases into the diagram. Use all the words from the box. The numbers in brackets refer to the pages in Prime Time 7 *where you can find these phrases. Only copy the phrases you can find there.*

high (p. 24) • important (p. 24) • increase (p. 22) • lead (p. 24) • linked (p. 24) •
needed (p. 25) • point (p. 21) • prevent (p. 26) • put (p. 25) • rely (p. 25) •
spend (p. 25) • suffer (p. 25) • turn (p. 24)

to

in
high

out

from

for

on

3 Prepositional phrases 2: Nutritional dilemmas

Use the prepositional phrases from task 2 on page 9 which fit best to fill in the gaps below.

Many modern diseases are ....*linked to*............ **(1)** the fact that many people tend to eat the wrong things at the wrong time. One of the consequences is that people .... **(2)** weight at an enormous rate, especially if they eat a lot of food that is .... **(3)** carbohydrates. Instead of .... **(4)** experts to get advice, the internet has .... **(5)** to be the source of information that is most .... **(6)** people struggling with their weight.

The rising number of obese people has led to a situation that is far from desirable. Even though one could argue that everybody is responsible for his or her well-being, experts .... **(7)** that the consequences are considerable for everybody as we – the tax payers – have to pay if there is an .... **(8)** health costs.

Governments should .... more money .... **(9)** advertisements to .... people .... **(10)** becoming overweight.

4 Research: Healthy eating

a) Do an internet search for the key words "healthy eating".
b) Choose at least two different sites and make a list.

What you should do	What you shouldn't do	What you should eat	What you shouldn't eat

5 Language in use: Advertising ban on smoking

You are going to read a text about an advertising ban on cigarettes. Some forms are missing from the text. Choose from the list (A–L) the correct part for each gap (1–9) in the text. There are two extra forms you should not use. Write your answers in the boxes provided. The first one (0) has been done for you.

In many countries, governments are discussing a ban on cigarette advertisements … **(0)** smoking is certainly one of the most harmful activities. … **(Q1)**, when you look at advertisements for cigarettes, smoking is usually presented as something … **(Q2)** provides freedom and is … **(Q3)** a form of expressing oneself. … **(Q4)** the positive feelings that are generated through advertising, smoking is a hazard and contributes enormously to rising health costs. A ban on smoking would immediately pay off … **(Q5)** it would reduce the number of people who suffer from lung cancer and other related diseases.

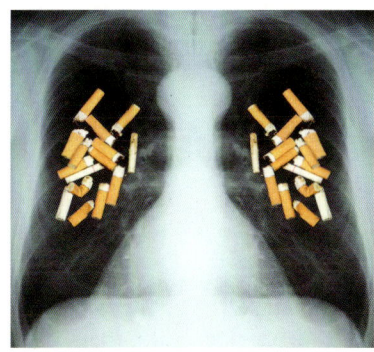

… **(Q6)** young people learn a lot about the negative effects of smoking in school, many teenagers take up smoking … **(Q7)** they think they are young and healthy … **(Q8)** nothing can harm them. Advertising contributes to this feeling as pictures are much more powerful than words. Printing health warnings on cigarette packs is one way of reminding smokers that their habit is detrimental to their health, … **(Q9)** young people tend to ignore these grim messages.

The countries which have imposed an advertising ban on smoking have shown the way. The question remains: Why don't the other countries follow?

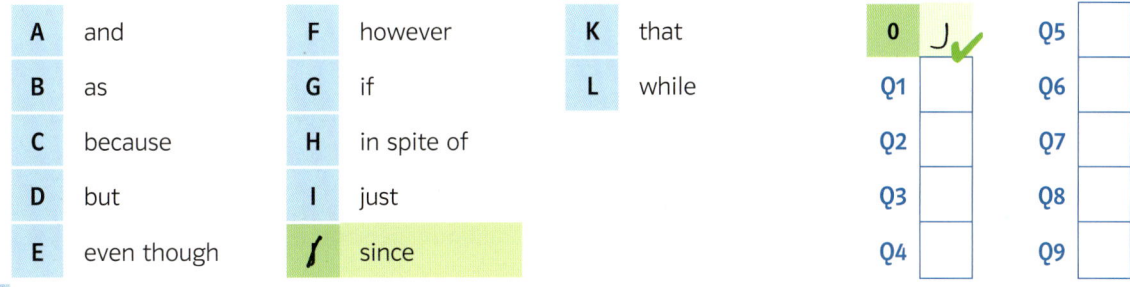

A	and	**F**	however	**K**	that	**0**	J ✔	**Q5**
B	as	**G**	if	**L**	while	**Q1**		**Q6**
C	because	**H**	in spite of			**Q2**		**Q7**
D	but	**I**	just			**Q3**		**Q8**
E	even though	**J**	since			**Q4**		**Q9**

6 Synonyms and antonyms

Read the text above again and find synonyms (s = words with the same meaning) and antonyms (a = opposites) for the words below.

1. bad for your health (s): ....*harmful*...

2. independence (s): ....

3. to be effective (s): ....

4. to increase (a): ....

5. to start (s): ....

6. harmful (a): ....

7. strong (s): ....

8. to help sb. forget (a): ....

9. to have a negative effect (s): ....

10. dreadful (s): ....

7 Smoking and health: Compound nouns

a) Choose words from the left and combine them with words from the right to form compound nouns.

1. blood	**C**	**A**	ache	
2. heart		**B**	rash	
3. immune		**C**	circulation	
4. lung		**D**	damage	
5. bone		**E**	organs	
6. skin		**F**	disease	
7. stomach		**G**	cancer	
8. oxygen		**H**	density	
9. arterial		**I**	substances	
10. osteoporosis		**J**	supply	
11. chemical		**K**	system	
12. reproductive		**L**	therapy	

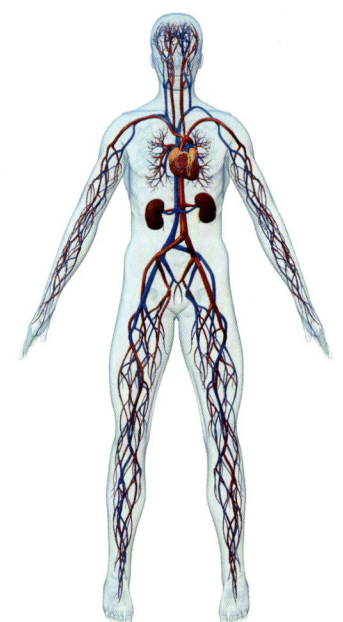

b) Research the usage of these words on the internet and copy one sentence with each of these compound nouns into your exercise book.

8 Word families

a) Fill the gaps with words from the same word family.

Verb	Noun (thing)	Noun (person)	Adjective
to educate	education	educator	educational
to			demonstrative
to	production/product		

b) With the help of a dictionary find more word families. If you can't find a word for a particular category, leave the space empty.

Verb	Noun (thing)	Noun (person)	Adjective
to smoke	smoke	smoker	smoking
to care			
to enjoy			
to	medicine/medication		
to sense			
to	society		
to use			

9 Word search: Living with disabilities

Find nine words related to the topic of "disabilities". The words may be written in all directions. There are two compound nouns.

	1	2	3	4	5	6	7	8	9	10	11	12
1	E	G	A	U	G	N	A	L	N	G	I	S
2	R	Q	H	S	D	I	S	A	B	L	E	D
3	A	G	P	A	S	V	Q	Q	V	C	J	E
4	T	F	D	T	S	I	P	A	R	E	H	T
5	I	T	S	R	L	Z	S	Y	M	A	V	N
6	E	A	N	O	I	T	A	T	I	M	I	L
7	M	K	T	N	E	M	R	I	A	P	M	I
8	T	L	I	P	R	E	A	D	I	N	G	O
9	H	E	A	R	I	N	G	A	I	D	C	J
10	R	E	S	T	R	I	C	T	I	O	N	E

10 Language in use: Dealing with people with disabilities in emergencies

You are going to read a text about helping people with disabilities. Some words are missing from the text. Fill in the word which best fits each gap (1–10). Use only one word in each gap. Write your answers in the spaces provided at the end of the text. The first one (0) has been done for you.

Dealing with people with disabilities can prove … **(0)** for first responders. The best way to go about it is to ask the person how you can best … **(Q1)** them. This is important because otherwise you might do things that are … **(Q2)** for the person you want to help. However, you have to make … **(Q3)** that the person has really understood what you have said. So take your time, be … **(Q4)** and listen carefully. 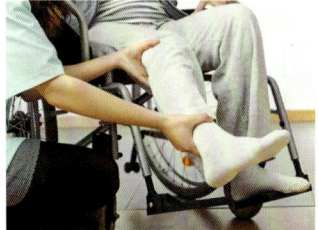 Sometimes people in … **(Q5)** situations may appear disoriented and confused. This may be due to their … **(Q6)**, e.g. a hearing loss or visual … **(Q7)**. In any case identify yourself, describe your situation and … **(Q8)** what you are doing. This may help the person to … **(Q9)** you and to cooperate where possible. Every person and every disability is unique. So the better you can adapt to the … **(Q10)**, the better it is for the disabled person and for you.

0	*challenging* ✔

Q1 ....

Q2 ....

Q3 ....

Q4 ....

Q5 ....

Q6 ....

Q7 ....

Q8 ....

Q9 ....

Q10 ....

Regional identities

1 What constitutes an identity?

a) Look at the following question posted in an internet discussion forum and write a short answer from your point of view.

Peggy
Total answers: 243

9:55 a.m.
Dear all,
I'm curious as to just what constitutes a person's identity and when someone has one.
　Is your identity something that one day you just have because you are born with it or is it something that you obtain and develop over time?

b) Now read what other people have answered. How do these answers differ from what you have written?

Randy
Total answers: 331

10:06 a.m.
Good question, Peg!
I think, identity is however a person chooses to define him-/herself.
　I guess all I'm wondering about is if someone's identity is something they have at one moment in their life and maintain or is it something that evolves over time?

Julie
Total answers: 89

11:59 a.m.
I have asked myself this question so often! I was adopted as an infant. I don't know if I had another name before or not and I've always known myself as Julie. I've always felt my identity as just what it is: the daughter of my parents.
　I feel that nature plus nurture plus life experience equals identity. It's both something you're born with and something you acquire. It evolves. Old parts of it fall away and new parts form. Maybe it is different for everyone.

Rick
Total answers: 152

2:09 p.m.
Dear all,
I think our experiences do contribute to who we are. We can choose our actions, which influence our character. We choose which goals we want to pursue. We're influenced by the people around us – family, friends, teachers, spouses, our own children, etc. All of that contributes to who we are and who we'll become.
　I believe you have to be very mature to stand for what you are and to like yourself. Your identity is just you, in every way. The way you are, you think, you live, you relate, you feel.

Millie
Total answers: 214

3:13 p.m.
Hi Peggy,
I decided that nobody has just one identity and it does not make sense to try and define it. To your co-workers you are someone, to your spouse you are someone else. When you are with your parents, you try to act the way they raised you. When you are around friends, you might want to prove that you are your own person by doing something that your parents would find very uncharacteristic of you.
　All the people around you can define who they think you are, they can give you an identity. But I believe it is impossible to give yourself an identity because you cannot decide when you are being the "real" you.

c) *Look at the words and definitions below and try to find a synonym for each of them in the forum postings.*

Word/Definition	Synonym
1. to create, establish	*to constitute*
2. to get, acquire	
3. to preserve, keep	
4. to develop, progress	
5. upbringing, education	
6. to affect emotionally	
7. to go after, follow	
8. one of a married couple	
9. adult, grown-up (adj.)	
10. out of the ordinary	

2 Regional identities

a) *Put the following words into the appropriate boxes. Which aspects of regional identity can you describe with them?*

~~adventurous~~ • agriculture • area • artistic • atheist • belief • bilingual • capital • ceremony • cheerful • Christian faith • church • continent • currency • dialect • district • education • energetic • entertainment • ethics • factory • faith • first language • fishing • flag • glacier • healthcare • helpful • hill • Hindu faith • impatient • independence • industry • information technology • interpret • Islamic faith • Jewish faith • kingdom • loyal • mass media • mining • monarch • mosque • mother tongue • mountain • native speaker • official language • optimistic • parliament • passionate • plain • pollution • pray • product • prosperous • recession • research • service sector • sociable • spiritual • state • stereotype • summit • synagogue • translate • transport • valley • value • village • war

Religion	
Geography	
People	*adventurous*
Language	
Traditions	
Economy	
History	

b) *Use appropriate words from above to describe the identity of your country, area or city. What is it like? What is important to you?*

3 Germanisms: 101 things to do in London

Cross out any of the words in brackets that are not correct. More than one option may be correct.

Kensington Roof Gardens: Atop the former Derry and Toms building high above Kensington High Street is this enchanting venue – a nightclub with 0.6 hectares of gardens. Formal dress code: (*smokings • dinner jackets*) (1) for men and long gowns for women.

Portobello Road Market: Perhaps because it's less crowded and littered than Camden, Londoners generally prefer this market. Though shops and stalls open daily, the busiest days are Friday, Saturday and Sunday. New shops selling men's underwear including T-shirts and (*briefs • slips • boxer shorts • underpants*) (2).

Shakespeare's Globe: The original Globe Theatre, where many of Shakespeare's plays were first staged, was dismantled in 1644. More than 300 years later, it was rebuilt not far from its original site, using construction methods and materials as close as possible to the ones initially used. Performances from April to October, no guarantee for a happy (*ending • end*) (3).

London Transport Museum: Among the vehicles on display at the London Transport Museum is the first underground electric train, which had no windows because there was nothing to see underground. Lots of (*oldtimers • vintage cars*) (4) on display!

Royal Opera House: Having secured its position as one of the world's greatest opera houses following a turn-of-the-century refurbishment, the Royal Opera House is ready for you. Don't forget to turn off your (*mobile • handy • cell phone*) (5) though!

4 False friends: Foras na Gaeilge

Choose the correct word in each pair and write the sentences down.

Irish Gaelic is one of three main languages of Ireland. Lately, unfortunately, it has been dwindling and almost disappeared. There is too much (*competition • concurrence*) (1) with English. Is Gaelic in danger of becoming extinct? Or is there hope?

One of the major (*actions • campaigns*) (2) dedicated to saving Irish is "Foras na Gaeilge". Since 1999, the "Foras na Gaeilge" has taken on the responsibility of promoting Irish throughout Ireland. It has an educational outline programme where being taught Irish from preschool through to third level is becoming more common in the local schools. Additionally, in the school cafeterias there is always one Gaelic (*daily special • menu*) (3) offered to students and staff.

Ireland also has Irish-only media sources in an effort to promote the language. The TG4 television (*channel • sender*) (4) produces programmes only in Irish. Experiments were carried out whether foreign language films could be (*dubbed • synchronised*) (5) in Irish. There are now three main newspapers that print (*only • consequently*) (6) in Irish. In radio there is "Raidió na Gaeltachta", while the BBC has started to air some programmes in Irish such as "Karen na hAoine".

If you aren't a citizen of Ireland there are other ways to either brush up on your Irish skills, or to learn Irish as a new language all on your own. A good workable software solution to learning Irish on your own is through the "Teach Me Irish!" language package. The (*parole • slogan*) (7) "Teach Me Irish!" stands for an interactive software programme that engages the student in proper pronunciation. This is (*carried out • realised*) (8) with voice-recognition feedback through the lessons. This programme also focuses on enabling the student to read Irish through twenty different stories that test the verbal word recognition already covered. Alternatively, there is also a "Rosetta Stone" Irish course to (*absolve • complete*) (9).

(Laura Jean Karr, *Bright Hub Education*, 20 February 2013; adapted and abridged)

5 **Language in use: Guide to California's Highway No. 1**

You are going to read a text about California's Highway No. 1. Some words are missing from the text. Choose from the list (A–L) the correct part for each gap (1–9) in the text. There are two extra words you should not use. Write your answers in the boxes provided. The first one (0) has been done for you.

There are a few great road trips that can … **(0)** almost anybody, a few that can instil a lifelong … **(Q1)** about what lies beyond the next turn. The road trip that made me love road trips was on Highway 1, also known as the Pacific Coast Highway, which stretches from Mexico to the town of Leggett in northern California but is perhaps most … **(Q2)** between Los Angeles and San Francisco.

As a kid, I took that 380-mile journey several times in the sixties and seventies, when my parents drove my older brother and sister to college in the Bay Area. Highway 1 was the road to freedom, and the trips were like … **(Q3)**, with the Lovin' Spoonful or the Doors on the radio, and the mist-shrouded mountains appearing like something out of Tolkien.

Of course, it's not only me. Highway 1 is the sort of road you see in car ads and movies, one that begs to be … **(Q4)** in a red convertible. It has stomach-dropping turns, wide, clean beaches and cliffs that plunge to the ocean. And just when you're thinking, "enough with the drama already", it offers up acres of soft green farmland – lettuce, strawberries, even the self-proclaimed artichoke capital of the world, Castroville. No wonder this highway is one of America's unofficial pilgrimage … **(Q5)** – for beatniks, surfers, food groupies chasing the latest fresh taste sensation and thrill-seekers of all sorts.

Last summer, when my husband and I took our East Coast-bred kids on a weeklong Highway 1 road trip from L.A. to San Francisco, I hoped that Ike, six, and Lucy, not quite three, would love it as I had. We decided to start off slowly with a two-night stop in Santa Barbara. Santa Barbara is one of those lucky places – lucky in its Mediterranean climate, its lemon- and lavender- and sea-… **(Q6)** air and its location, nestled between the Santa Ynez Mountains and a curve of coastline where palm trees lean toward the sea. It was even lucky, in a way, in the earthquake that destroyed the town in 1925, … **(Q7)** its civic fathers to build a planned city such as you rarely see in the United States, with a lot of red-tile-roofed Spanish Colonial … **(Q8)**.

On Stearns Wharf the first evening, we found a funky little novelty confection store, where we bought candy lipstick and gummy penguins. Ike and Lucy ate them while we looked back at the mountains … **(Q9)** straight and misty blue in the twilight, their foothills dotted with glimmering lights.

Want to know how our road trip continued? Make sure to return next week to our second part of the series.

(Travel and Leisure, April 2014; adapted and abridged)

A	allowing	**F**	driven	**K**	scented	
B	architecture	**G**	forceful	**L**	streets	
C	captivating	**H**	movies			
D	charm	**I**	rising			
E	curiosity	**J**	routes			

0	D ✓
Q1	
Q2	
Q3	
Q4	
Q5	
Q6	
Q7	
Q8	
Q9	

6 Language in use: Go Midwest, young writer

a) *You are going to read a text about the American Midwest. Some words are missing from the text. Choose from the list (A–L) the correct part for each gap (1–9) in the text. There are two extra words you should not use. Write your answers in the boxes provided. The first one (0) has been done for you.*

For many people, New York is the publishing … **(0)** of the country, and a lot of people who write do live in Brooklyn. I can totally … **(Q1)** up everything you've heard about thriving independent bookstores, nightly literary … **(Q2)** and writers crowding the coffee shops. Yet, New York City isn't the only place to be if you're a writer. A closer look at the literary map of the 50 states … **(Q3)** that some of the most exciting things going on in American literature are taking place in the middle of the country.

The Midwest is a region that offers a terrain nearly as … **(Q4)** as its cultures. There's BBQ in Kansas City, and you eat your weight in cheese curds in Milwaukee; Nebraska has corn, Michigan has cars; people from St Paul sound like they could be from Canada; you might mistake people from Indiana for southerners because of their … **(Q5)**. The Midwest is the place where industry lives and dies, politics are life, and people have a thousand stories to tell like they're coming down a swiftly-moving conveyer belt. It's also getting pretty hard to deny, as … **(Q6)** rents continue to rise in places like Brooklyn, that the Midwest, with its free houses for writers in Detroit, great university towns and neighbourhoods like Ann Arbor, Hyde Park and Iowa City, might really be ready to … **(Q7)** over as the place for writers to call home.

The middle of the country still receives its share of pitying glares from the publishing world. No matter how much … **(Q8)** is made, there will always be people who think the middle of the country is just a place you fly over.

How can you think so little of the Midwest when you take into consideration everything that is coming out of places like Ohio, Illinois, Michigan and Iowa? Writers like Kyle Minor, Roxane Gay and Adam Levin, literary journals like *PANK*, the presses like Graywolf, Two Dollar Radio and Curbside Splendor – all of these things make it hard to … **(Q9)** that the Midwest has become a region of serious literary importance. Combine all that with the fact that the cities are actually livable, and it might not be long until you start seeing trend pieces declaring the Midwest the new American literary hot spot.

(Jason Diamond, *Flavorwire*, 24 March 2014; adapted and abridged)

A	accents	**F**	epicentre	**K**	reveals	**0**	F ✓	**Q5**	
B	astronomical	**G**	events	**L**	take	**Q1**		**Q6**	
C	back	**H**	ground			**Q2**		**Q7**	
D	deny	**I**	make			**Q3**		**Q8**	
E	diverse	**J**	progress			**Q4**		**Q9**	

b) *Look at the words and definitions below and find a synonym for each of them in the text above.*

Word	Synonym	Word	Synonym
1. prosperous, growing	thriving	**5.** quickly, rapidly	
2. autonomous		**6.** feeling sorry	
3. landscape		**7.** gaze, look	
4. to confuse, mix up sb.		**8.** popular place	

Adolescence

1 **Synonyms**

Find synonyms for the words (1–16) in the box below. Use a dictionary if you are not sure what these words mean.

> inestimable affectionate
> positive calm lively good-looking
> infinite perpetual joyful sincere
> honourable authentic beautiful
> faithful self-sacrificing ~~tender~~

1. compassionate: ......*tender*...

2. devoted: ....

3. divine: ....

4. endless: ....

5. eternal: ....

6. fond: ....

7. genuine: ....

8. honest: ....

9. merry: ....

10. noble: ....

11. optimistic: ....

12. peaceful: ....

13. precious: ....

14. selfless: ....

15. stunning: ....

16. vibrant: ....

2 Language in use: Becoming sophisticated

You are going to read a text about a typical problem of teenagers. Some words are missing from the text. Choose the correct answer (A, B, C or D) for each gap (1–10) in the text. Write your answers in the boxes provided. The first one (0) has been done for you.

Has it ever crossed your mind that you would like to appear as a sophisticated adult? What seems to be something out of reach can be … **(0)** easily if you follow these guidelines.

The first thing is to be polite and … **(Q1)**. But how on earth should you be able to do that? The answer is simple: Just lean back and listen to what other people want to tell you. Show your … **(Q2)** in what they are saying by looking into their eyes and by asking intelligent questions or making intelligent … **(Q3)** – but not too many. Sometimes it might be enough just to say, "Hhmm." "Aha." "Oh yeah."

Make sure your behaviour fits the etiquette of the group you want to belong to. Certain rules and … **(Q4)** behaviour is required if you want to belong to a social group. The faster you can adapt to these unwritten rules, the better. … **(Q5)** as you should will make other people feel more comfortable and ultimately they will like your company. However, social rules depend on the cultural background of a specific group. So it makes … **(Q6)** to watch and listen first before you make a bold move.

Be aware that people watch you. So make sure you read quality papers and magazines and let other people see what you are doing. A positive side-effect might be that you can … **(Q7)** enough general … **(Q8)** to appear sophisticated. The saying "You are what you read" shows the importance of one's reading matter.

But most important of all, be respectful. This goes down well with everybody. But that also means that you are aware of your own strengths and … **(Q9)**.

If you follow these … **(Q10)** you can be sure that people will see you as a sophisticated adult, a person to talk to, somebody who shows respect.

(Billy Stone et al., *www.wikihow.com*; adapted and abridged)

0	A	acted upon	B	infused	¢	achieved	D	got
Q1	A	charmed	B	thrilled	C	excited	D	charming
Q2	A	meaning	B	knowledge	C	interest	D	interaction
Q3	A	wordings	B	comments	C	opinions	D	sayings
Q4	A	specific	B	specified	C	special	D	species
Q5	A	Making	B	Behaving	C	Moving	D	Doing
Q6	A	sense	B	meaning	C	opinion	D	sensation
Q7	A	attract	B	find out	C	collect	D	acquire
Q8	A	wisdom	B	know	C	purpose	D	knowledge
Q9	A	weakness	B	weaklings	C	weaknesses	D	weakliness
Q10	A	rulers	B	guidelines	C	guides	D	guidance

0	Q1	Q2	Q3	Q4	Q5	Q6	Q7	Q8	Q9	Q10
C ✔										

3 Teenagers behaving badly – How parents see it

Read through the text below, highlight the important passages and then fill in the grid with arguments for both sides.

When children become teenagers, they want to break away from their parents because they think that they need to be independent. This situation may be exciting for teenagers and also
5 worrying, but this time is at least as confusing for them as it is for their parents.

At times parents have the feeling that their son or daughter has changed so much that they fear they cannot communicate with their
10 children.

What worries parents most is the fact that many teenagers start hiding their private lives from them. Instead of talking about their school life or about their friends, teenagers start making up stories or do not even speak to them at all.

15 One of the reasons might be that teenagers need to try out things which their parents would never allow them to do. Such risky behaviour can lead to enormous problems even though in most cases nothing really worrying happens. It may be that parents are so suspicious of their teenage children because they remember what they did when they were the same age.

As teenagers see themselves as responsible adults, they cannot understand that their parents
20 want to interfere. What follows are endless arguments about rules and the right behaviour, sometimes ending in fierce discussions and disrespectful behaviour on both sides.

So, what is the best advice for parents of teenagers? The best way to deal with "problem" children is probably to relax and to wait until things have changed. Most teenagers do become responsible adults sooner or later, in spite of their parents' attempt to educate their children. Just
25 give them time to find their own identity.

What teenagers do or want to do	What parents do or want to do
• Teenagers want to break away from home.	

4   Phrasal verbs

a) Read the story "First love" on page 52 in Prime Time 7 *again and look out for phrasal verbs.*

b) Match the phrasal verbs in the box with the words and phrases (1–18) below.

be around • be up • break up • build up • call for • catch on • come out with •
come up to • get up • go for • go off • go on • go out with boys/girls •
happen to • meant for • take out • ~~turn out~~ • wait for

1. prove to be: ......*turn out*...

2. leave one's bed in the morning: ....

3. leave: ....

4. develop: ....

5. come near: ....

6. go and ask for sb.: ....

7. escort sb. to a social event: ....

8. declare oneself: ....

9. intended for: ....

10. occur by chance: ....

11. spend time with boys/girls: ....

12. continue: ....

13. await: ....

14. end a relationship: ....

15. become aware: ....

16. go on: ....

17. like: ....

18. be in the same place as oneself: ....

c) Now go back to page 52 in Prime Time 7 *and find the phrasal verbs from the box in the story.*

5 Mixed conditionals, part 1: Difficult teenage years

Read the text below and fill in the missing forms. Use the words in brackets.

If parents ....*remembered*............ (**1 remember**) how they behaved when they were young, they would not be too strict with their teenage children. Their children, on the other hand, should also learn that they need to treat adults with respect if they .... (**2 want**) to have a pleasant and peaceful life. If both sides .... (**3 realise**) early enough that they need to respect each other and give each other enough freedom and space to breathe and develop, things will hopefully soon turn out to be unproblematic.

However, if parents .... (**4 want**) their children to grow up and become independent adults, they should be aware that it takes a lot of patience and trust to cope with this difficult situation.

In most cases, communication is a key factor. Things could easily get out of control if parents and children .... (**5 stop**) talking, or even if they just .... (**6 argue**), but at least in this case there .... (**7 be**) some form of communication.

And what .... (**8 shall, do, they**) if something goes wrong? If something unexpected or worrying .... (**9 happen**), teenagers and their parents should stay calm and try to start over. But this does not always work, as we all know.

For my part I can say, had my parents tried to understand me when I was fourteen, I .... (**10 have**) fewer problems at school and also in later life.

6 Mixed conditionals, part 2

Read the sentences below and fill in the missing forms. Use the words in brackets.

1. If I ....*had met*............ (**meet**) him earlier, he would now be the company chairman. But I didn't, bad luck for him.

2. If our car .... (**be stolen**), I would have called the police. But our car wasn't stolen and so there was no need to call the police.

3. If we had seen her last week, she .... (**know**) that we have no time to come round tomorrow.

4. If I .... (**speak**) Chinese back then, I could have translated the text for her.

5. We would now be able to get in, if he .... (**order**) the tickets in time.

6. I am sure he would call me if he .... (**find**) out something new. It seems he hasn't.

Extreme situations

1 Extreme word wheel

Word wheels are easy to build and help you to keep track of all the words you should know. You just need some cardboard and a paper clip.

a) Make yourself a word wheel by following the instructions below.

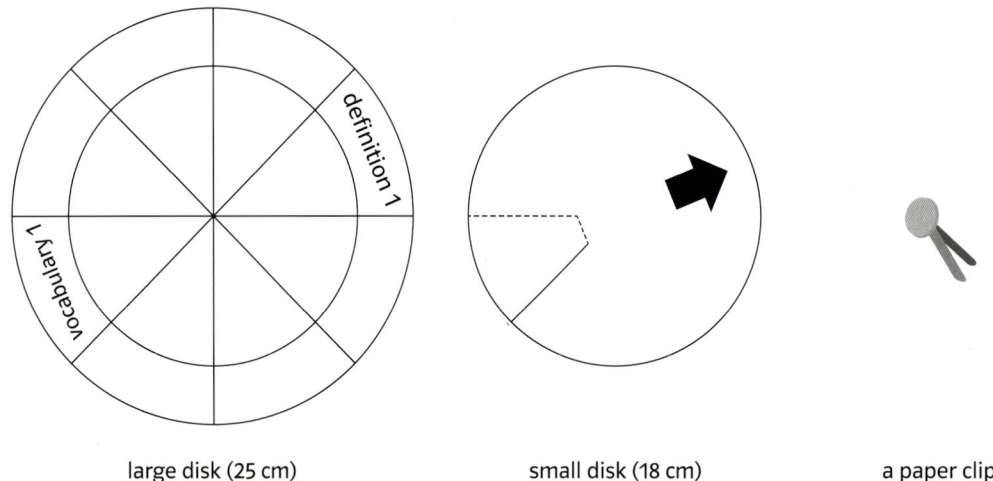

large disk (25 cm)   small disk (18 cm)   a paper clip

- *First, draw a circle of 25 centimetres on one piece of cardboard and cut it out. Divide it into eight sections as shown.*
- *After that, draw a second circle of 18 centimetres on a separate piece of cardboard and cut it out.*
- *Cut out the window on the small disk on the dotted lines and fold it on the solid line.*
- *Draw an arrow on the other side as shown above.*
- *Put the small disk on top of the large disk and attach them with a paper clip in the middle.*

b) Now pick eight words you want to study from below.

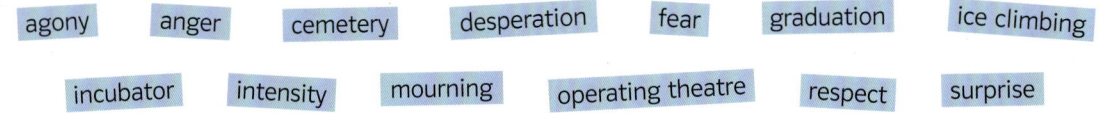

agony   anger   cemetery   desperation   fear   graduation   ice climbing

incubator   intensity   mourning   operating theatre   respect   surprise

- *Write a definition of the first word into one of the eight sections on the outer rim of the large disk.*
- *After that, fold back the window and write down the word itself.*
- *Repeat these steps until all eight words have definitions.*

c) Now study the words using your word wheel.
- *Turn the wheel so that the arrow points to a definition. The correct word will appear in the window.*
- *To test yourself, close the window on the word wheel.*
- *To check, fold back the window.*

d) Fill in suitable words from above into the sentences below.

1. John Hunter Hospital's .... are understaffed by 37 full-time nurses.

2. It was a weekend of emotional tributes, physical .... and heartbreaking defeats.

3. The University of Derby has confirmed that its next .... ceremonies will go ahead.

4. About 25 tombstones were toppled during a spree of vandalism at Elmwood ....

5. .... is a modern sport adding a new dimension to the Olympic Games.

2 Language in use: Too much school stress may make kids sick

You are going to read a text about the effect of stress on young people. Some words are missing from the text. Choose the correct answer (A, B, C or D) for each gap (1–10) in the text. Write your answers in the boxes provided. The first one (0) has been done for you.

Could too much homework become … **(0)** to your child's health? In a recent TV documentary, several teens reported they were feeling overwhelmed due to lots of homework, high … **(Q1)** to get good grades and, ultimately, get into college.

Fourteen-year-old freshman Natalie stated she was already feeling the heavy … **(Q2)**. "When you get a ton of homework assignments and if you feel that you don't do all of them perfectly, and you're already worrying in your freshman year that you're not going to get into college, it causes you to panic," she said.

The stress is taking a … **(Q3)** on students, not only emotionally, but physically too. "My heart starts beating really fast and I get really nervous wondering how am I going to get all of this done in … **(Q4)**?" Natalie added.

Some students revealed they were spending hours completing piles of homework. "I get home maybe around 6, I stay up until midnight doing homework, and then I get up at 6 a.m. to do more homework," Natalie declared. This, of course, … **(Q5)** little time for anything else, including sleep.

Researchers at Stanford University recently said the number of teens seeking therapy to help manage this stress is on the … **(Q6)**. "We're seeing increased pressures to get into college. We have young kids in 9th grade contemplating what they're going to do with their lives. They're so … **(Q7)** with having to make these decisions and the competition," said Talia Filippelli, of Starr Psychotherapy.

Filippelli revealed that depression, anxiety, moodiness, nervousness, stomach aches, headaches, and exhaustion were the most … **(Q8)** effects of school stress. Parents can help by managing their own stress levels. "Parents living high-stress lives don't realise that their kids are actually mirroring and … **(Q9)** the way they handle stress," Filippelli said. For children and teens who aren't able to manage their stress while in school, it may … **(Q10)** to other stress-related illnesses when they get older, including obesity, diabetes and heart disease.

(www.newyork.cbslocal.com, 24 March 2014; adapted and abridged)

0	A	risky	B	painful	C	destructive	Ø	harmful
Q1	A	demands	B	requests	C	interests	D	pursuits
Q2	A	benefit	B	hardship	C	difficulty	D	burden
Q3	A	payment	B	toll	C	expense	D	value
Q4	A	punctuality	B	deadline	C	time	D	moment
Q5	A	denies	B	has	C	leaves	D	makes
Q6	A	boost	B	progress	C	growth	D	rise
Q7	A	excited	B	touched	C	overwhelmed	D	moved
Q8	A	common	B	popular	C	routine	D	everyday
Q9	A	cloning	B	copying	C	doing	D	making like
Q10	A	introduce	B	lead	C	pass	D	set up

0	Q1	Q2	Q3	Q4	Q5	Q6	Q7	Q8	Q9	Q10
D ✓										

3 How Christopher McCandless died

Read the article on the death of Christopher McCandless.

On 6 September 1992, the body of Christopher McCandless was discovered by moose hunters in a rusting bus just outside the northern boundary of Denali National Park. Taped to the
5 door was a note. It said: "I need your help. I am injured, near death, and too weak to hike out of here. I am all alone, this is no joke. In the name of god, please remain to save me. I am out collecting berries close by and shall return this
10 evening."

From a cryptic diary found among his possessions, it appeared that McCandless had
15 been dead for nineteen days. A driver's license issued eight months before he perished indicated that he was
20 twenty-four years old and weighed a hundred and forty pounds. An autopsy determined that he weighed sixty-seven
25 pounds and lacked subcutaneous fat. The probable cause of death, according to the coroner's report, was starvation.

In my book *Into the Wild* I came to a different conclusion. I've speculated that
30 McCandless had poisoned himself by eating seeds from a plant commonly called wild potato. According to my hypothesis, a toxic agent in the seeds must have weakened McCandless to such a degree that it became
35 impossible for him to hike out to the highway or hunt, leading to starvation.

McCandless's diary shows that beginning on 24 June 1992, the roots of the wild potato plant became a staple of his daily diet. On July 14th, he
40 started harvesting and eating the seeds as well, to make up for his caloric deficit due to his marginal diet of squirrels, small birds, mushrooms, roots and berries. After July 30th, his physical condition deteriorated, and three
45 weeks later he was dead.

The wild potato was universally believed to be safe to eat. Tests taken after McCandless's death didn't reveal any toxic agents in the plant and so some scientists believed the adventurer had mistaken poisonous plants with the
50 seemingly harmless wild potato. Recently, a writer named Ronald Hamilton posted a thoroughly researched paper on the internet that brought new facts to the discussion. The toxic agent in the wild potato turned out to be
55 an amino acid, and according to Hamilton it was the chief cause of McCandless's death.

In the meantime, Hamilton's findings have
60 been backed up by chemical analysis: wild potato seeds contain the substance ODAP. ODAP was identified in 1964. It
65 brings about paralysis by over-stimulating nerve receptors, causing them to die. Occasional consumption of food
70 containing ODAP as one component of an otherwise balanced diet bears no risk of toxicity. Experts warn, however, that individuals suffering from malnutrition, stress, and acute hunger are especially sensitive to
75 ODAP, and are thus highly susceptible to its paralysing effects.

As McCandless exactly matched the profile of those most susceptible to ODAP poisoning, it might be said that he did indeed starve to death
80 in the Alaskan wild, but this only because he'd been poisoned, and the poison had rendered him too weak to move about.

Had McCandless's guidebook to edible plants warned that wild potato seeds contain a
85 neurotoxin that can cause paralysis, he probably would have walked out of the wild in late August with no more difficulty than when he walked into the wild in April, and would still be alive today. If that were the case,
90 Christopher McCandless would now be in his mid-forties.

(Jon Krakauer, The New Yorker, 12 September 2013;
adapted and abridged)

4 Conditions

Imagine the journalist who wrote the article on page 26 is being interviewed for a TV documentary on Christopher McCandless. Complete the journalist's answers using a suitable form of the conditional.

Interviewer: Shortly before his death, Christopher McCandless taped a note on the door of his bus. What might have happened if the note had been found earlier?

Journalist: .... **(1)**

Interviewer: Contrary to the coroner's report and public opinion you speculated that McCandless had poisoned himself by eating seeds of the wild potato plant. What would have happened if he hadn't eaten the seeds?

Journalist: .... **(2)**

Interviewer: Why did McCandless actually add the wild potato plant to his diet? What was the danger he might have run into had he continued eating just squirrels, small birds and mushrooms?

Journalist: .... **(3)**

Interviewer: In the meantime it was found out that the wild potato plant does contain a toxic agent, a substance called ODAP. What happens to the body if this substance is ingested?

Journalist: .... **(4)**

Interviewer: How about if I consumed food containing ODAP occasionally? I am healthy and have a rather balanced diet. What would happen to me?

Journalist: .... **(5)**

Interviewer: What might actually have happened had Christopher McCandless's guidebook to edible plants warned him that wild potato seeds can cause paralysis?

Journalist: .... **(6)**

5 Comparisons

Form sentences using the comparative and the superlative that refer to the article on page 26.

1. McCandless • find • weigh • little • healthy person of his age

   When McCandless was found, he weighed less than a healthy person of his age should.
2. Jon Krakauer • speculate • eating wild potato seeds • make • McCandless • weak • from day to day

   ....
3. People • believe • wild potato plant • safe • many other vegetables

   ....
4. Maybe • Ronald Hamilton • careful • research • other investigators in McCandless's death

   ....
5. According to Hamilton • wild potato plant • important • cause • McCandless's death

   ....
6. ODAP • dangerous • many other types of poison

   ....
7. weak and stressed people • threatened • by ODAP • people with a balanced diet

   ....

6 Language in use: My parents chose my husband

You are going to read a text about an arranged marriage. In most lines of the text there is a word that should not be there. Write that word in the space provided after each line. Some lines are correct. Indicate these lines with a tick (✔). There are two examples at the beginning.

When I tell people here in America that I have an arranged marriage **advice**, they	*advice*	0
react in one of two ways. Some love my story because it appears to confirm their	✔	00
belief that America is doing it the wrong: "Kids nowadays – having sex in	....	Q1
middle school! All the single mums! The institution of marriage is dying! Your	....	Q2
popular culture is just so beautiful." Others are more cautious. If Alex happens	....	Q3
to be around, they appraise us both, searching for signs of trauma centre or	....	Q4
misery. Eventually, they did lean in and whisper, "Well, it ended up just fine,	....	Q5
right? You're both happy? You've made it to work and it was all for the best?	....	Q6
Right?" These aren't really questions. They're statements which designed to	....	Q7
make everything OK, and I know my cue well enough by now to smile and	....	Q8
say, "Yes! – Yes, of course." The "yes" is not exactly a lie detector. Alex and I	....	Q9
have been married for 17 years, and our relationship is a stable. But the life we	....	Q10
live together is still difficult for me to accept with. For one thing, the words	....	Q11
"arranged marriage" conjure up images that have nothing left to do with me.	....	Q12
Child brides and dowry burnings on the one hand, or henna and Bollywood on	....	Q13
the other. I grew up in the USA, a product test of New England suburbia,	....	Q14
evangelical Christianity and Wellesley College. I was the bicultural kid brother	....	Q15
who wore salwar kameezes during the day, read Sweet Valley High at night and	....	Q16
swooned over "happily ever after" stories. But I always knew with my marriage	....	Q17
would be arranged. Dating was absolutely forbidden in my family. By the time I	....	Q18
turned 20, I knew my arranged marriage was set in stone fruit. Saying "no"	....	Q19
(though I still longed to) was not for an option. The stakes in our honour-and-	....	Q20
shame-based family tree were too high, even though this is hard to understand.	....	Q21

India

1 **Finding useful expressions: India**

Go through the words below and put two together to form compound nouns. The first one has been done for you. Look up the words you don't know.

British legacy, ...

....

....

....

....

....

....

2 **Finding the right meaning**

Match the expressions on the left with words on the right.

1. rich	F	**A**	diligent
2. to bring up		**B**	poor
3. causing worries		**C**	mosque
4. lots of money		**D**	to raise
5. to become smaller		**E**	caste
6. hard-working		**F**	affluent
7. social class in India		**G**	small fortune
8. poverty-stricken		**H**	disturbing
9. to realise		**I**	to shrink
10. Muslim place of worship		**J**	to become aware

3 Language in use: Connectives – Elections in India

You are going to read a text about elections in India. Some words are missing from the text. Choose the correct answer (A, B, C or D) for each gap (1–10) in the text. Write your answers in the boxes provided. The first one (0) has been done for you.

General elections in India are a major challenge to organisers and voters alike … **(0)** India is the biggest democracy in the world. In 2014 about 814 million people had the right to vote. Among them were 20 per cent first-time voters … **(Q1)** made the outcome even less predictable. … **(Q2)** only between 50 and 60 per cent of the voters take part in these elections, the number of votes to be counted is still enormous. Around five million people are required to conduct the procedure and another five million are needed to make sure … **(Q3)** the election procedure is fair and proper.

… **(Q4)** cope with the vast size of the country, voting takes place in nine phases spread out over six weeks. … **(Q5)** the elections are in progress, voting commissions travel the country to carry out the polls.

At the end of this procedure 543 members of the lower house will be elected. Each MP represents one constituency … **(Q6)** is elected through a majority system, … **(Q7)** means that only the votes cast for the winner are counted.

… **(Q8)** the fact that India seems quite chaotic for Westerners the democratic system seems to work. … **(Q9)**, voting is one thing but ruling the country in a fair way is … **(Q10)** important.

0	A	while	B	whereas	**C**	as	D	despite
Q1	A	what	B	which	C	that	D	while
Q2	A	As	B	Because	C	Even though	D	When
Q3	A	that	B	because	C	although	D	since
Q4	A	In order to	B	Because of	C	For	D	When
Q5	A	After	B	Before	C	Since	D	While
Q6	A	also	B	and	C	or	D	even
Q7	A	what	B	which	C	therefore	D	so
Q8	A	Because of	B	As	C	In spite of	D	For
Q9	A	However	B	Moreover	C	Similarly	D	Likewise
Q10	A	as well as	B	likewise	C	equally	D	likely

0	Q1	Q2	Q3	Q4	Q5	Q6	Q7	Q8	Q9	Q10
C ✔										

4   Language in use: The caste system

You are going to read a text about the social system in India. Some words are missing from the text. Use the words in brackets to complete each gap (1–16) in the text. Write your answers in the spaces provided at the end of the text. The first one (0) has been done for you.

Society in India is divided into castes based on the ancient Hindu system of four groups according to their … **(0 spirit)** and physical … **(Q1 develop)** and self-control. These four groups or castes were … **(Q2 close)** associated with the function individuals had in society: The highest caste, the Brahmins, were regarded as the intellectual and spiritual guides, as priests and philosophers. The second group were the Kshatriyas, the caste of warriors and … **(Q3 rule)**. Then came the Vaishyas, mostly … **(Q4 trade)**, and … **(Q5 labour)** and craftsmen made up the lowest caste, the Shudras.

Higher castes did not mix with people from lower castes, as they did not want to spoil their family … **(Q6 rank)**. In order to keep up this rigid caste system people who broke the … **(Q7 rule)** had to face severe … **(Q8 punish)**.

When Britain ruled India, they tried to … **(Q9 strong)** the rights of the lower castes and to ban traditional practices that were … **(Q10 accept)** for the British, but most of these attempts were … **(Q11 success)**.

Since the … **(Q12 adopt)** of the Constitution of India in 1949 all Indian citizens share the same rights.

However, in spite of the changes in the law, the most important influence on the current social system has been the … **(Q13 economy)** boom of the last few years. Megacities have emerged and the traditional social system started to crumble. In … **(Q14 add)** to that the opportunities provided by the thriving economy have made it possible to become successful outside the barriers of social traditions. … **(Q15 Gradual)** the system is changing but many of the social … **(Q16 divide)** of Indian society can still be observed around the country.

0	*spiritual* ✔

Q1 ....

Q2 ....

Q3 ....

Q4 ....

Q5 ....

Q6 ....

Q7 ....

Q8 ....

Q9 ....

Q10 ....

Q11 ....

Q12 ....

Q13 ....

Q14 ....

Q15 ....

Q16 ....

5 Language in use: Mohandas Karamchand Gandhi – The Great Soul

You are going to read a text about Mohandas Karamchand Gandhi. Some words are missing from the text. Choose from the list (A–N) the correct part for each gap (1–11) in the text. There are two extra words you should not use. Write your answers in the boxes provided. The first one (0) has been done for you.

Mohandas Karamchand Gandhi was India's most … **(0)** leader before the country became independent in 1947. Originally he was trained as a lawyer and worked in England and – after a brief period in India – he went to South Africa where he … **(Q1)** racial discrimination. His reaction was non-violent action against the authorities in order to help … **(Q2)** the situation of Indians in South Africa. Back in India again, he became a very influential leader of the … **(Q3)** movement. His strategy of non-violence and non-cooperation with the government was the secret of his success. Over the years he … **(Q4)** his strategies. One of his actions was to … **(Q5)** a "Salt March" with thousands of supporters. They walked to the sea to produce their own salt from the seawater as the British Government had the salt monopoly and had put … **(Q6)** taxes on salt.

In his political … **(Q7)** he also fought for the rights of women, of poor farmers and labourers, and against the Indian caste system.

In his later life he was … **(Q8)** as a spiritual and a political leader. One of his aims was to stop the Hindu-Muslim conflict on the Indian subcontinent, which ultimately led to his … **(Q9)**. He could not … **(Q10)** the creation of India as a mainly Hindu state and Pakistan (which later split into Pakistan proper and Bangladesh) as Muslim territories.

What is most interesting about Mohandas Karamchand Gandhi is the fact that in the western world he is a highly respected spiritual leader whereas people in India have … **(Q11)** about him.

A	activation	**G**	independence	**M**	regarded	**0**	K ✓	**Q6**	
B	assassination	**H**	mixed views	**N**	stage	**Q1**		**Q7**	
C	career	**I**	movement			**Q2**		**Q8**	
D	experienced	**J**	prevent			**Q3**		**Q9**	
E	heavy	**K**	prominent			**Q4**		**Q10**	
F	improve	**L**	refined			**Q5**		**Q11**	

6 Synonyms and antonyms

Read the text about Gandhi again and find synonyms (s = words with the same meaning) or antonyms (a = opposites) for the words and phrases below.

1. self-governing (s): ....

2. unfair treatment (s): ....

3. plan of action (s): ....

4. opponents (a): ....

5. money paid to the state (s): ....

6. formation (s): ....

7. to separate (s): ....

8. countries (s): ....

7 Language in use: Bollywood

You are going to read a text about Bollywood. Some words are missing from the text. Use the words in brackets to complete each gap (1–12) in the text. Write your answers in the spaces provided at the end of the text. The first one (0) has been done for you.

Bollywood – a … **(0 combine)** of Bombay and Hollywood – is a PR term which is often mistaken for the Indian movie industry as a whole. In fact it is only one strand of Hindi cinema which … **(Q1 origin)** in the Parsi theatre tradition. The Indian movie industry has developed outside the Hollywood tradition, but who would doubt the impact of a term like Bollywood.

Most of the films produced in Mumbai (which is modern-day Bombay) are in Hindi, Urdu or Hindustani languages, with an increasing influence of English, as the market for Indian-made movies keeps … **(Q2 grow)**. In terms of films … **(Q3 release)** and tickets … **(Q4 sell)** Bollywood is the biggest movie industry worldwide even though it lags far behind Hollywood … **(Q5 financial)** as tickets in India and the rest of Asia are very cheap compared to ticket prices in Europe and the US.

However, more and more films from India are sold to cinema companies around the world in order to provide Indian and Pakistani communities with this form of … **(Q6 entertain)**. These films are also … **(Q7 popularity)** with audiences in Iran, Afghanistan and the Middle East. As a consequence the movie industry has become an important export factor for India.

… **(Q8 origin)** the quality of Indian movies was rather poor compared with American or European films, but gradually the Indian film industry is catching up.

Hindi films are usually very … **(Q9 colour)** and contain music and dance scenes which are normally written … **(Q10 specific)** for these movies. Experts point out that these elements were also … **(Q11 type)** of American movies in the 1950s as they also featured songs and dance scenes to support the plot and to add to the atmosphere.

Nowadays also TV series and soap operas are produced in Mumbai, turning the actors and actresses into celebrities with an enormous … **(Q12 follow)**.

0	*combination* ✔

Q1	....	Q7	....
Q2	....	Q8	....
Q3	....	Q9	....
Q4	....	Q10	....
Q5	....	Q11	....
Q6	....	Q12	....

Celebrities

1 **Too many talent shows on TV in China?**

The Voice of China, Chinese Idol and *Happy Boys* are just a few of the many talent shows on television today. However, this may soon change with the announcement of restrictive regulations by the Chinese State Administration of Press, Publication, Radio, Film and Television (SAPPRFT).

According to SAPPRFT, there are too many such talent shows on television, which are similar in concept as well as content. So SAPPRFT announced that it would implement regulations on the nation's singing competition shows to "avoid monotony among programmes, provide more options to the audience and satisfy diverse demands." Moreover, it points out that all television programmes must "avoid extravagance, luxury, sensationalism and flashy programming."

a) *There are supporters of and opponents to this idea. First, have a look at the keywords below and fill in the word which best fits each gap.*

administrative   audience's   broadcasting   choice   ~~copycat~~   excellent   improve

opportunities   ratings   standards   thrive   uncover   unpopular

			+	?	–
1. competition • audience ratings • large number of ....*copycat*.......... programmes			☑	☐	☐
2. provide .... • once unknown singers • follow their dreams			☐	☐	☐
3. measures • help • coordinate • .... times of these singing shows			☐	☐	☐
4. producers must realise • not everyone • interested in • larger			☐	☐	☐
5. excessive production • waste of resources • waste of .... time			☐	☐	☐
6. good TV shows • preserved • .... ones • gradually be eliminated			☐	☐	☐
7. singing contest programmes • .... • many talented singers			☐	☐	☐
8. stay within law and social moral .... • tolerance should be given			☐	☐	☐
9. weekends • always • given to talent shows • highest audience			☐	☐	☐
10. authorities • unable • order all TV channels • produce .... programmes			☐	☐	☐
11. many TV programmes • manage to .... • despite regulation and control			☐	☐	☐
12. best way out • not .... interference • market rules			☐	☐	☐
13. competition • TV channels • motivated to .... • better programmes			☐	☐	☐

b) *Now tick the plus sign (+) to mark an opinion as positive, the question mark (?) to mark it as neutral and the minus sign (–) to mark it as negative towards SAPPRFT's plans.*

c) *Now write two statements: one in favour of the regulations, and one opposing it. Use the ideas presented above and techniques to connect ideas and to contrast opposing views.*

2 Language in use: How to know all the latest celebrity gossip

You are going to read an article about keeping up to date with celebrity gossip. Some words are missing from the text. Use the words in brackets to complete each gap (1–16) in the text. Write your answers in the spaces provided at the end of the text. The first one (0) has been done for you.

Celebrity gossip isn't just about what celebrities are up to and who's dating whom. It's also about music, fashion, sports and trends. Your favourite band released a new album … **(0 expect)**? Drew Barrymore is wearing Vera Wang? Tiger Woods did what? Being up to date on the latest celebrity gossip can make you the life of the party. Don't let yourself put at a … **(Q1 advantage)**! But isn't it … **(Q2 realistic)** to keep up with all the gossip? No! This guide will tell you how to save money and time and become an expert at anything celebrity-related.

Invest in some magazines. There are heaps of magazines in which you can read all the latest gossip about what's going on in the celebrity world. Don't just read such magazines every couple of days; read them every day. Do you find yourself near a newsstand? Take your time to look at the covers and maybe flick through the pages to stumble upon even the most … **(Q3 significant)** story. You will soon find the attraction of celebrity news … **(Q4 resistible)**. Yet, if you are … **(Q5 willing)** to spend money on gossip, there are a number of free alternatives!

Watch entertainment shows on TV. It's … **(Q6 lead)** to say that the days of the television are over. You can get fairly new gossip on your television every day. There's a lot that you can choose from, and it can be pretty convenient if you just want to sit back and relax, watching gossip … **(Q7 stop)**. … **(Q8 like)** with tabloids, you don't have to pay for the whole thing when you just want one story. You can tune in to the parts you want to hear and switch the channel when you feel like it.

Start reading celebrity gossip sites. The good thing about gossip sites is that they are constantly updated. You can read articles that were just released and see candid celebrity pictures from an hour ago. In contrast to magazines and TV, though, the web is mostly … **(Q9 censored)** – so you might also find one or the other … **(Q10 tasteful)** story or … **(Q11 appropriate)** content. If it's too … **(Q12 convenient)** for you to visit the websites regularly you can add an RSS feed, sign up for newsletters or get alerts. That way, you'll know when something big happens right away.

Meet the stars. Are you afraid that you are being … **(Q13 informed)** by the media? That there's dirt that you'll never read about? When you actually encounter a star, you get to have a close-up of their fame and personality for a few moments. Don't be … **(Q14 patient)** – you will meet your favourite star eventually. Many stars actually like being talked to and are … **(Q15 happy)** if they are not recognised. Update your friends with "real-life" gossip that's exclusive only to you but don't forget to ask the celebrity for permission to post or publish photos to avoid doing something … **(Q16 legal)**.

0	*unexpectedly* ✔

Q1 .... Q9 ....

Q2 .... Q10 ....

Q3 .... Q11 ....

Q4 .... Q12 ....

Q5 .... Q13 ....

Q6 .... Q14 ....

Q7 .... Q15 ....

Q8 .... Q16 ....

3 Opposites, opposites

a) *Write down the opposite forms of the words below and arrange them in groups according to their prefix.*

> ~~able~~ • accurate • to activate • adequate • afraid • to agree • appropriate • available • aware • capable • certain • clear • compatible • complete • to construct • flexible • friendly • helpful • to inform • known • legal • legible • literate • logical • loyal • mature • patient • perfect • pleasant • pleased • possible • realistic • regular • relevant • resistible • responsible • secure • significant • sufficient • to trust • visible

un-	de-/dis-	im-/in-	ir-	il-
unable				

b) *Fill in appropriate forms from the table above.*

1. More infants are ……*unable*……… to play with building blocks because they're too addicted to iPads.

2. Two men were arrested on Thursday for allegedly being in ……………………………… possession of firearms.

3. It was discovered recently that increased CO_2 levels make fish ……………………………… of predators.

4. The health department warned that five helpings of fruit and vegetables a day is still ………………………………. You definitely need to eat more.

5. State transportation officials are asking Jersey City to temporarily ……………………………… the red-light camera at Newark Avenue.

6. Despite the various literacy programmes implemented in recent years, more than half of the Moroccans aged 15 and older are ……………………………… and can't even read simple signs.

7. US Airways has apologised for posting an ……………………………… image of a woman on Twitter, but the internet won't be forgetting about it anytime soon.

8. We instinctively ……………………………… phone calls that tell us we have won a free vacation or car.

9. Due of the world economic crisis India's entrepreneurs face an ……………………………… future.

10. The biggest hazard in morning traffic is ……………………………… motorists driving their cars onto pavements in an attempt to get around dustbin lorries.

4 Learning vocabulary: Recording vocabulary

When you encounter new vocabulary, you need to use various techniques to help yourself remember the word. First, though, you need to decide how important the word is for you. It is a good idea to collect as much information as possible about the word such as:

- the meaning of the word
- how to spell it
- how to pronounce it
- grammatical information about the word (noun, verb, adjective, etc.)
- which phrases it typically occurs in (collocations)
- which other words it is related to (word family)
- how the word is made up (what other words or affixes are part of the word)
- example sentences

You can record this information in notebooks, on word cards or on your digital devices.

a) *Below you can find example entries of eight words related to the film industry. Match the words and the correct additional information from the table in a notebook or on notecards. Pay special attention to the column on the right ("related word"). These words belong to the same lexical field as your main entry. The related words help you to expand your vocabulary and understand in which context your main entry is usually used.*

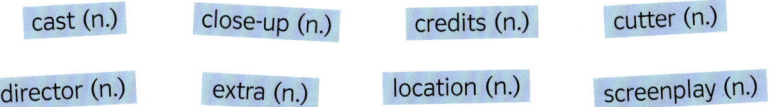

cast (n.)   close-up (n.)   credits (n.)   cutter (n.)

director (n.)   extra (n.)   location (n.)   screenplay (n.)

Definition	Typical phrase	Lexical field	Related word
1. movie shot taken at close range	Alright, I'm ready for my … .	camera angles	bird's eye
2. person engaged to fill out a crowd scene in a film	Looking for male … aged 27 to 35.	members of a film cast	actor
3. person editing a film after the shoot	The … works closely with the director.	members of a film crew	camera operator
4. actors in a film production	The actor joined the … of "Ant-Man".	types of job in film-making	crew
5. person supervising the actors in a film	The … is known for the biggest box-office hits of all time.	members of a film crew	script supervisor
6. list of people involved in the production	There is a basic order for a film's closing … .	parts of a film	opening sequence
7. script for a film or TV programme	You have to write the … in the correct industry format.	documents for film production	music score
8. place of production outside of the studio	The film was shot entirely on … in Sweden.	setup of a movie scene	lighting

b) *Collect three more related words for each of the eight entries and copy them into your list.*

c) *Collect vocabulary related to another topic the way shown above and make yourself familiar with this method for recording vocabulary.*

5 Language in use: Attack of the paparazzi

You are going to read an article about the daily life of a paparazzo. Some words are missing from the text. Use the words in brackets to complete each gap (1–12) in the text. Write your answers in the spaces provided at the end of the text. The first one (0) has been done for you.

Vladimir Labissiere sits off Sunset Boulevard in his new black Mercedes E350. He spends a lot of time in alleys waiting for his shots. The 40-year-old Vlad is a pap, short for paparazzo, the despised shooters who bring you all the pictures and videos you say you loathe but … (0 **actual**) stare at online for hours. He's one of … (Q1 **hundred**) in L.A., trying to make a living on anywhere from $10,000 to $150,000 a year by photographing every move an A-, B- or even D-lister … (Q2 **make**). Some of the stars hate them, some of the stars use them in a now-estimated billion-dollar business, where millions of … (Q3 **consume**) scan websites, magazines and television shows for the … (Q4 **tiny**) scrap of information.

Vlad is one of them. Right now, he's waiting for British pop star Jessie J to emerge and head to a nearby recording studio. Vlad checks her Instagram page and sees that she's at the rooftop pool, so it will be a while. Paps live on situational … (Q5 **aware**) – a … (Q6 **six**) sense anticipating what is going to happen next.

It's not an easy life, being a pap, and it's getting harder. New legislation went into effect in California on January 1ˢᵗ, preventing paps from shooting children in an … (Q7 **alarm**) manner based on their parents' fame. This was bad news for the paps, since mum-and-kid shots sell best.

A little after 1:00, Jessie J … (Q8 **final**) appears. An SUV pulls out of the hotel and Vlad follows. Jessie J is in the back seat. He trails her to Record Plant Studios, overtaking her car so he can arrive a minute or two early and set up. He's already on the sidewalk and shooting when a … (Q9 **secure**) guy asks him to let Jessie's mum pass. Vlad agrees and then shoots Jessie wearing a wig and a tired smile. "Jessie's huge in England," he says. "I'll shoot her every day, and I'll have a complete story to sell. It's not about one picture – it's about the whole story."

He drives away, but quickly turns his car around as he sees a white Range Rover drive by and recognises the license plate. "Yeah, '047'. It's January Jones!" The best paps have memorised hundreds of license plates. Some celebs know it and … (Q10 **constant**) switch cars. Vlad claims he's seen Harry Styles driving half a dozen … (Q11 **differ**) vehicles. Vlad might make about $500 for an exclusive Jones shot, but could make twice that for one with her kid. The Rover pulls up to a house in a nondescript (Q12 **neighbour**). Vlad can see a toddler in a car seat. Nothing happens for a while. Eventually, Vlad breaks off the chase, reasoning Jones is heading home to Los Feliz, and that won't work.

(Stephen Rodrick, *Rolling Stone*, 17 April 2014; adapted and abridged)

0	*actually* ✔

Q1	....	Q7	....
Q2	....	Q8	....
Q3	....	Q9	....
Q4	....	Q10	....
Q5	....	Q11	....
Q6	....	Q12	....

Art

1 **Artists**

Study the expressions below and write them into the correct box. Some words can be written into more than one box. Look up the words you don't know.

actor/actress author ballet dancer cartoonist choreographer
composer conductor designer director DJ dramatist
entertainer graphic designer illustrator lyricist musician
novelist painter playwright poet scriptwriter sculptor
singer soloist songwriter storyteller
VJ vocalist writer

Performing arts and music	Visual arts	Literature
actor/actress		

2 Finding the right meaning

Match the words on the left with the correct definitions or examples on the right.

1. to abandon	I	**A**	show
2. art gallery		**B**	spray painting on walls
3. art scene		**C**	to present (e.g. an opening ceremony)
4. boundary		**D**	to appear suddenly
5. exhibit		**E**	place where pieces of art are exhibited and sold
6. to go mainstream		**F**	act of breaking the law
7. graffiti		**G**	picture created by
8. to host		**H**	to apply a liquid in small drops
9. offence		**I**	to give up completely, to stop looking after
10. painting by		**J**	social group which focuses on buying, selling and admiring art
11. to pop up		**K**	artist using public places as his/her gallery
12. to spray		**L**	act of deliberate destruction
13. street artist		**M**	to become accepted
14. vandalism		**N**	dividing line

3 Language in use: What the artist says

You are going to read a text in which an artist talks about his views. Some words are missing from the text. Choose the correct answer (A, B, C or D) for each gap (1–18) in the text. Write your answers in the boxes provided. The first one (0) has been done for you.

… **(0)** me, art is like a lifestyle. What I prefer is to capture what already exists. That means that … **(Q1)** my images I capture emotions, ideas, memories. My favourite art form is video which enables me to combine what I see and hear … **(Q2)** multiple ways.

When I sit … **(Q3)** home and work … **(Q4)** my computer I can arrange and rearrange what I have collected – the images, the sounds, the movements. And even though I've been doing that for several years now I keep finding new ways of expressing myself. … **(Q5)** combining the material I have found and recorded I create something new, something inspiring. … **(Q6)** other words I explore the world … **(Q7)** the moving images and the results can be shared … **(Q8)** exhibitions.

But I don't only produce videos, I also collect artefacts and objects found … **(Q9)** location to create three-dimensional sculptural collages, which reflect the atmosphere in a more direct way. These pieces can be exhibited … **(Q10)** my video clips and can be accompanied by sound recordings. Sometimes I even add texts, which are either presented in the videos or put … **(Q11)** the objects I make.

My art is deeply personal. It is the result of a process that goes … **(Q12)** in my mind and is only reflected … **(Q13)** the objects and videos I produce. It is my way … **(Q14)** interpreting the world as I see it. It is an urge which I cannot stop; I simply have to do what I am doing.

However, everyone who looks … **(Q15)** my pieces has to make sense of what I am doing … **(Q16)** a personal level. I can only present my views, others have to judge and evaluate what they think … **(Q17)** my activities.

As far as I am concerned life … **(Q18)** art would be meaningless.

0	**A**	With	**B**	On	**C̸**	To	**D**	In
Q1	A	on	B	in	C	for	D	without
Q2	A	upon	B	in	C	on	D	at
Q3	A	at	B	in	C	on	D	up
Q4	A	for	B	in front of	C	upon	D	at
Q5	A	In	B	By	C	For	D	With
Q6	A	In	B	At	C	By	D	For
Q7	A	for	B	on	C	through	D	by
Q8	A	on	B	in	C	from	D	for
Q9	A	in	B	by	C	on	D	with
Q10	A	next	B	alongside	C	by	D	for
Q11	A	in	B	during	C	next to	D	for
Q12	A	up	B	for	C	within	D	on
Q13	A	upon	B	for	C	in	D	up
Q14	A	to	B	for	C	at	D	of
Q15	A	in	B	at	C	on	D	out of
Q16	A	on	B	in	C	for	D	under
Q17	A	with	B	from	C	of	D	by
Q18	A	with	B	without	C	on	D	for

0	Q1	Q2	Q3	Q4	Q5	Q6	Q7	Q8	Q9	Q10	Q11	Q12	Q13	Q14	Q15	Q16	Q17	Q18
C✓																		

4 Language in use: The Guggenheim Museum Bilbao

You are going to read a text about the Guggenheim Museum in Bilbao. Some words are missing from the text. Use the words in brackets to complete each gap (1–14) in the text. Write your answers in the spaces provided at the end of the text. The first one (0) has been done for you.

What Philip Johnson called "the … (**0 great**) building of our time" is … (**Q1 doubt**) one of the most stunning constructions ever built. … (**Q2 situation**) in urban Bilbao, the Guggenheim Museum was part of a much larger re-development programme that was created to revive an industrial city that had suffered … (**Q3 consider**) under the collapse of the traditional industrial base in the 1980s and 1990s. The companies which had brought enormous wealth to the area – large steel mills and shipyards – had to close down and what was left were the sites of these icons of … (**Q4 industry**).

In order to combat this industrial downturn a massive … (**Q5 invest**) programme was started which – among other things – led to the … (**Q6 construct**) of a museum of modern art in … (**Q7 cooperate**) with the Guggenheim Foundation. Frank O. Gehry, a Californian architect, was commissioned to design the building, and he chose to create a structure that looks most … (**Q8 spectacle**) because of its use of various materials, among them steel, glass and titanium, which accounts for the silver skin of the facade.

Today the building houses a permanent … (**Q9 exhibit**) of modern and contemporary art … (**Q10 span**) from the great names of the first half of the 20th century to young, upcoming Spanish and Basque … (**Q11 art**).

Since its … (**Q12 open**) in 1997 the Guggenheim Museum in Bilbao has become the … (**Q13 dominate**) visual feature of Spain's fourth largest city making it a major tourist … (**Q14 attract**) and an important art venue with worldwide appeal.

0	greatest ✔

Q1	....	Q8	....
Q2	....	Q9	....
Q3	....	Q10	....
Q4	....	Q11	....
Q5	....	Q12	....
Q6	....	Q13	....
Q7	....	Q14	....

5 Language in use: Confusable words – Abstract art

You are going to read a text about abstract art. Some words are missing from the text. Choose the correct answer (A, B, C or D) for each gap (1–13) in the text. Write your answers in the boxes provided. The first one (0) has been done for you.

… **(0)** abstract art can be found almost everywhere. In some … **(Q1)** it is fashionable to own an abstract painting or … **(Q2)** a good reproduction of one. However, it seems to be the focal point of discussions over and over again as it can be … **(Q3)** or challenging. It is the fact that abstract art is non-representational that leads to negative reactions. … **(Q4)** all these discussions we ought to remember that abstract art was first created to represent the changes in the real world towards the end of the 19th century. So, in a way, it was an attempt to come to … **(Q5)** with the world but today the situation has changed.

As abstract art is widespread, many people feel unable to deal with it. Some don't like it, others … **(Q6)** it, or they are simply disappointed that in spite of their … **(Q7)** they don't understand it.

Another aspect is certainly the fact that talking about abstract art is … **(Q8)** more difficult than talking about art that mirrors the real world in the form of people and objects that can be … **(Q9)** as what they are.

Yet, once you've become … **(Q10)** to typical features of abstract art and as soon as you have stopped … **(Q11)** about the message an abstract piece of art should convey, the form, the colours, the shapes, the lines, the texture, etc. can be … **(Q12)**.

However, beauty is in the eye of the beholder, as the saying goes – and the same … **(Q13)** to art.

0	A	Now	B	In those days	C	Nowadays	D	Yet
Q1	A	rounds	B	cycles	C	circles	D	rings
Q2	A	at last	B	at least	C	lastly	D	least
Q3	A	provident	B	provoked	C	provocative	D	provisional
Q4	A	Because of	B	In spite of	C	During	D	By
Q5	A	terminals	B	terminus	C	thermals	D	terms
Q6	A	despise	B	depict	C	depart	D	depose
Q7	A	efforts	B	effects	C	affects	D	affords
Q8	A	deniably	B	undenied	C	denied	D	undeniably
Q9	A	recognised	B	realised	C	related	D	relayed
Q10	A	customised	B	accustomed	C	accumulated	D	custodial
Q11	A	wondered	B	interfering	C	wondering	D	questioning
Q12	A	intrigued	B	intricate	C	intriguing	D	intrigue
Q13	A	appals	B	applied	C	appalled	D	applies

0	Q1	Q2	Q3	Q4	Q5	Q6	Q7	Q8	Q9	Q10	Q11	Q12	Q13
C✓													

Ethnic and cultural diversity

1 Bias and stereotyping

Lazy. Seductive. Intelligent. Used to describe individuals, these adjectives pose no particular problem. Used to describe groups of people, however, they may constitute stereotypes. Stereotypes are qualities assigned to groups of people related to their race, nationality or sexual orientation. Because they generalise groups of people in manners that lead to discrimination and ignore the diversity within groups, stereotypes should be avoided.

Both negative and positive stereotypes exist, but even the latter do harm. That's because all stereotypes are limiting and leave little to no room for individuality. Perhaps a child belongs to a racial group known for being highly intelligent. This particular child, however, suffers from a learning disability and struggles to keep up with his classmates in school. Because his teacher believes in the stereotype that this child is supposed to excel in class because "his people" are highly intelligent, she might assume that his poor marks are because he's lazy.

(Nadra Kareem Nittle, *About.com*; adapted and abridged)

a) Below you will find a number of stereotypes. Sort them into one of the four categories: age, culture, gender and other.

1. Absolutely all teenagers are rebels.

2. Virtually every American is obese and dim-witted.

3. Elderly people frequently forget where they have put their glasses.

4. Asian people are always good at maths.

5. Generally speaking, men are messy and unclean.

6. Basically, no politician thinks of the benefit of society.

7. It's normal for children to hate healthy food.

8. Most librarians are elderly women with glasses.

9. Girls are almost never good at sports.

10. Men are usually stronger than women.

11. Punks are definitely a menace to society.

12. There is no doubt that all English people only drink tea.

	Age	Culture	Gender	Other
1				

b) Study the examples in detail and find out which particular words or phrases are used to turn these sentences into stereotypes.

c) Go online and collect more phrases to express generalisations.

d) Use the phrases below to make sentences in which you contradict the stereotypes (see task 1a).

It is not conclusively proven …		
We cannot confidently predict …		
It is not well-documented …		… because … .
We cannot safely assume …	that	… as can be seen … .
There is considerable doubt …		… which is shown by … .
It is highly uncertain …	if	… which is exemplified by … .
It is controversial …		… which is illustrated by … .
It is debatable …	whether	… for example … .
It is on shaky foundations …		… for instance … .
It is an unjustified assumption …		
There are unfounded rumours …		

2 Racial (in)equality

Racism has existed throughout human history. It may be defined as the hatred of one person by another, or the belief that a person is inferior to others because of their skin colour, language, customs, place of birth or any factor that supposedly reveals the basic nature of that person. It has influenced wars, slavery, the formation of nations and legal codes.

Contemporary scientists do not agree on whether race is a valid way to classify people. What may seem to be significant "racial" differences to some people like skin colour, hair or facial shape are not of much scientific significance. In fact, genetic differences within a so-called race may be greater than those between races.

a) Look at the word spider showing various types of racism. Copy the correct labels next to the definitions below.

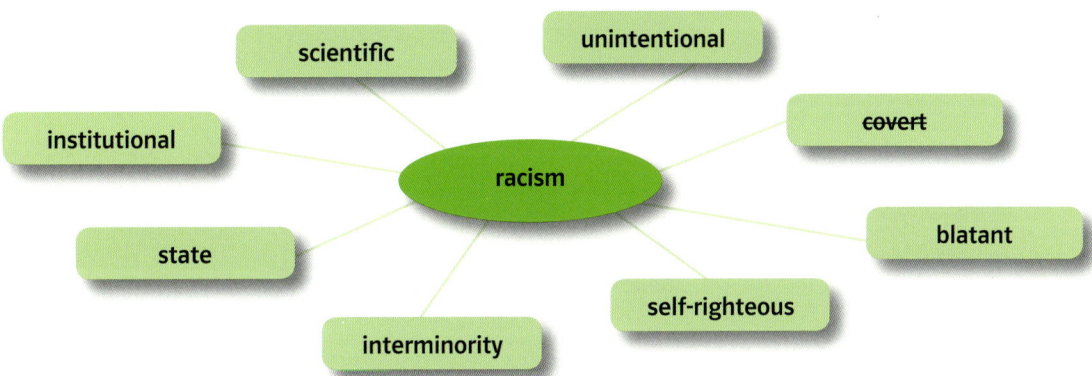

1. ………covert………: behaving in a racist way towards others but not telling people openly

2. …………………………: apologising for racism that happened before and being racist in doing so

3. …………………………: practices of a nation that are grounded in racist ideology

4. …………………………: telling people of a certain community what issues they have to deal with

5. …………………………: use of (pseudo)scientific ideas and concepts to justify racist ideas

6. …………………………: as a rule, certain rights or benefits are denied to certain groups of people

7. …………………………: prejudiced thinking among and between minority groups

8. …………………………: telling people openly that due to their cultural background they are inferior

b) Fill in the appropriate words into the table below. Each word is the opposite of one expression in the first column.

discrimination   favourite   immigration   ~~minority group~~

segregation   tolerance   uniformity

Word	Opposite
1. majority group	*minority group*
2. prejudice	
3. affirmative action	
4. emigration	
5. scapegoat	
6. integration	
7. diversity	

c) Complete the sentences with suitable words from task 2a on page 45 and from above.

1. One only needs to look at the propaganda posters of World War II to see the ....*blatant*............ racism, with the Japanese depicted as rats and snakes.

2. Apple Inc. has said it wants more ethnic .... in the basic range of emoji available to text-messaging apps.

3. White people tended to interact predominantly with other .... group members, and were more likely to "stick together".

4. A recent study reveals that .... racism begins as early as preschool. In US public schools, black students are more likely to get suspended than any other race.

5. Mexicans were being used as .... for the lack of jobs and resources at the time.

6. You often hear people say that we don't have a .... problem and that people live where they want to live regardless of their skin colour.

7. Proponents of .... in admissions say the policies help create more diverse campuses, which better prepares all students for life after school.

8. .... racism is racism that is subtle and not always obvious to an observer. It is much harder to fight against than more obvious forms of racial discrimination.

9. The Irish have a long history of .... but only recently has Ireland turned to those who have left the country.

10. One of Britain's best young tennis players is suing the game's governing body over claims his career has been damaged by racial ....

d) Go online and look for more example sentences in which these expressions appear.

3 Language in use: Diwali – The festival of lights

You are going to read a text about the Hindu Diwali festival. Some words are missing from the text. Fill in the word which best fits each gap (1–12). Use only one word in each gap. Write your answers in the spaces provided at the end of the text. The first one (0) has been done for you.

Diwali, the Hindu festival of lights, is the most popular of all the festivals originating in South Asia. It extends over five days and is a great favourite … **(0)** children because of the lights, fireworks and sweets involved. The festival celebrates the victory of good over … **(Q1)**, light over darkness and knowledge over ignorance. What the festival of lights … **(Q2)** for today is a reaffirmation of hope, a renewed commitment to friendship and goodwill, and a celebration of the joys of life.

    In Britain, as in India, the festival is a time for thoroughly spring-… **(Q3)** the home, wearing new clothes and, most importantly, decorating buildings with fancy lights. The British city of Leicester is well-known for its Diwali celebrations with … **(Q4)** to 35,000 people attending the switch on of the lights on Belgrave Road and even more attending Diwali day itself in the heart of the city's Asian community.

    The name of the festival comes from the Sanskrit word "dipavali", meaning row of lights. On that occasion, houses, shops and public places are decorated with small oil lamps made of clay called diyas. These lamps, which are traditionally … **(Q5)** by mustard oil, are placed in rows in windows, doors and outside buildings to decorate them. The lamps are lit to help the goddess Lakshmi find her way into people's homes. In India oil lamps are often floated across the river Ganges – it is regarded as a good omen if the lamp manages to get all the … **(Q6)** across. Fireworks are a big part of the Diwali celebrations, although in recent years there has been a move … **(Q7)** them because of noise and pollution and the number of accidental injuries and even deaths.

    The … **(Q8)** on which Diwali is celebrated is set by the Hindu calendar, so it varies in the Western calendar. It usually falls in October or November. Business people regard it as a favourable day to … **(Q9)** a new accounting year because of the festival's association with Lakshmi, the goddess of wealth. Many Indians see Diwali as an occasion to gamble. This comes from a legend in … **(Q10)** the goddess Parvati played dice with her husband on this day and said that anyone who gambled on Diwali night would do well.

    Diwali is very much a time for buying and exchanging gifts. Traditionally sweets and dried fruit were very common gifts to exchange, but the festival has … **(Q11)** a time for serious shopping, leading to anxiety that commercialism is eroding the spiritual side of the festival. In most years shopkeepers expect sales to rise substantially in the weeks … **(Q12)** the festival.

(*www.bbc.co.uk*, 20 October 2010; adapted and abridged)

0	with ✔

Q1	....	Q7	....
Q2	....	Q8	....
Q3	....	Q9	....
Q4	....	Q10	....
Q5	....	Q11	....
Q6	....	Q12	....

4 The history of Ellis Island

a) Highlight the conjunctions, time expressions, etc. typically used with tenses expressing past meaning.

For over 60 years, Ellis Island was the gateway for millions of immigrants to the United States. From 1892 to 1924, it was America's largest and most active immigration station, where over twelve million immigrants were processed.

It has been estimated that close to 40 per cent of all current US citizens can trace at least one of their ancestors back to Ellis Island. On average, the inspection process took approximately three to seven hours. For the vast majority of immigrants, Ellis Island was an "Island of Hope" – the first stop on their way to new opportunities and experiences in America. For some, though, it became the "Island of Tears" – a place where families were separated and individuals were denied entry into the country.

Ellis Island opened to the public in 1976. Today, visitors can tour the Ellis Island Immigration Museum in the restored Main Arrivals Hall and trace their ancestors through millions of immigrant arrival records made available to the public in 2001. In this way, Ellis Island remains a central destination for millions of Americans seeking a glimpse into the past of their country, and, in many cases, into their own family's history.

b) Complete the second part of the text with the correct past forms of the verbs given.

When Ellis Island ....opened............ **(1 open)**, a great change .... **(2 take)** place in immigration to the United States. More and more immigrants .... **(3 pour)** in from southern and eastern Europe due to war, drought, famine and religious persecution. All .... **(4 have)** hopes for greater opportunity in the New World.

After an exhausting sea voyage, the immigrants .... **(5 tag)** with information from the ship's registry and .... **(6 pass)** through long lines for medical and legal inspections to determine if they .... **(7 be)** fit for entry into the United States. Those who .... **(8 refuse)** entry to the United States .... **(9 have)** to remain on the island. Legal detainees .... **(10 get)** the chance to have their case reviewed a few days later. People who .... **(11 detain)** for medical reasons .... **(12 care)** for at the island's hospital or .... **(13 keep)** in quarantine. Eventually, a Board of Special Inquiry .... **(14 decide)** whether to allow them into the United States.

After they .... **(15 pass)** medical and legal inspections, the immigrants .... **(16 arrive)** at the top of another staircase at the other end of the Great Hall. At the bottom of the stairs .... **(17 be)** a post office, a ticketing office for the railways, an office to exchange money from their home country for US dollars, and social workers to help the immigrants who .... **(18 need)** assistance. An area on the first floor of the building .... **(19 become)** known as "the kissing post". It .... **(20 get)** that nickname because there family and friends .... **(21 wait)** for their loved ones.

Shakespeare live

Combine the verbs from the word cloud with the nouns in the table below. Some verbs can be used with more than one noun. The first one has been done for you.

make publish watch paint write raise earn join found choose take direct create

Verb	Noun
1. *to take, to create*	a role
2.	a portrait
3.	a living
4.	a topic
5.	a play
6.	a theatre
7.	a performance
8.	a book
9.	an actors' company
10.	a script
11.	money
12.	a character

2 Finding alternative expressions

The following text passages have been taken from Prime Time 7, *unit 10. Match the phrases below (1–11) with phrases from these text passages. Then rewrite the sentences with the alternative phrases.*

- 1587: Shakespeare has established himself in London as an actor and playwright. (p. 140)
- Apart from religious issues, Elizabeth had to deal with conspiracies, outbreaks of the plague, threats of invasions by France and Spain, and fighting in Ireland and the Netherlands. (p. 141)
- The best actors, directors and studios would be at his disposal – and we would see him in advertisements for computers, cologne, anti-balding creams and anti-hunger campaigns: "All the world's a stage for helping the developing world." (p. 142)
- Stars such as Al Pacino, Kenneth Branagh and Emma Thompson have dedicated years of their careers to the world's most venerated writer, while generations of new fans have been won at the box office. (p. 142)
- Indeed, nearly anything associated with Shakespeare turns to gold. (p. 142)
- In this era of visual overkill, it seems increasingly important to be able to put a face to the name. So what did Shakespeare actually look like? (p. 142)
- At one time it had also belonged to Sir William Davenant, a playwright who claimed that he was Shakespeare's illegitimate son. (p. 143)
- It cannot be said for sure what he did to earn a living for his small family. (p. 144)
- In 1612 Shakespeare returned to Stratford, where he bought some land and was involved in a few lawsuits. (p. 144)
- Various contemporaries of Shakespeare have been suspected of being the true author of the plays, among them Christopher Marlowe, a young and highly talented poet and Cambridge graduate; Edward de Vere, Earl of Oxford, a man of great learning and wealth; and even Queen Elizabeth herself. (p. 144)
- The case for the Earl of Oxford is based on the idea that a nobleman at the time could not very well be associated with the theatre as actors had such a low reputation. (p. 144)

Paraphrase	Original phrase in text passage
1. to find one's position in life; to set up a home	to establish oneself
2. to cope with	
3. to be available for	
4. to give time to; to devote time and effort to	
5. to be linked to	
6. to identify	
7. to be owned by	
8. to have enough income	
9. to be engaged in; to have to deal with	
10. to be believed to be	
11. to rest on	

3 Life at the Globe Theatre

a) Look at the sentence halves below and complete them with what you know about the Globe Theatre. Study the texts on pages 146 and 147 in Prime Time 7 *if you are short of ideas.*

The building

The Globe Theatre had the shape of … .
The centre of the theatre was … .
The theatre was made of … .
The roof was … .
A flag on the roof of the theatre indicated … .

The plays

The plays were written for … .
They included … .
Shakespeare wrote about … .
Shakespeare's plays were published … .
Plays were usually performed … .

The actors

The plays were performed only … .
The parts of the ladies were … .
The actors had to speak … .
Actors were members … .

The stage

The stage was open … .
When actors were on stage, they stood … .
There was no … .
Above the stage there was … .

The props and costumes

Hardly any props were … .
Actors had to describe … .
Costumes were often chosen … .
An actor with a lantern meant that … .

The audience

People in the audience were allowed to … .
They paid … .
They often … .
They even threw things at the actors if … .

---

b) Combine the sentences from the task above to create a well-rounded text about the Globe Theatre. Use linking words where necessary.

4 Language in use: Celebrating Shakespeare's Birthday

You are going to read a text about the way in which Shakespeare's birthday is celebrated. In most lines of the text there is a word that should not be there. Write that word in the space provided after each line. Some lines are correct. Indicate these lines with a tick (✓). There are two examples at the beginning.

For more than 200 years **time** Stratford-upon-Avon has been celebrating	....time....	0
Shakespeare's birthday on the weekend closest to April 23ʳᵈ, which is said to	✓	00
be of Shakespeare's date of birth. However, his correct date of birth	....	Q1
will never be known well, but experts believe that he must have been	....	Q2
born around this time of the year as he was baptised on 26 April 1564.	....	Q3
During these annual celebrations, tourists from all over the world come to	....	Q4
Stratford and take part time in the festivities. Some events are run by	....	Q5
the Royal Shakespeare Company and the Shakespeare Birthplace Trust	....	Q6
and include poetry readings, song music and drama performances	....	Q7
and special skills programmes at the five houses which are associated	....	Q8
with William Shakespeare.	....	Q9
A procession through the historic leisure centre of Stratford is the highlight	....	Q10
of the festivities which ends in the Holy Trinity of Church where Shakespeare	....	Q11
was buried alive in 1616.	....	Q12
In addition, visitors can watch street entertainers, listen to horror story tellers	....	Q13
or take part in theatre make-up artist activities for children. And if you are	....	Q14
lucky you might see a famous actor or two celebrating Shakespeare's	....	Q15
birthday in the town where he was never born.	....	Q16
However, Shakespeare's hometown is not the only town to celebrate	....	Q17
his birthday certificate. There are numerous places all over the world where	....	Q18
local Shakespeare companies put on performances or other events to	....	Q19
commemorate and to pay money tribute to the greatest British poet	....	Q20
and playwright of all times favourite.	....	Q21

5 Language in use: Sam Wanamaker – The man who revived the Globe Theatre

You are going to read a text about the actor Sam Wanamaker. In most lines of the text there is a word that should not be there. Write that word in the space provided after each line. Some lines are correct. Indicate these lines with a tick (✓). There are two examples at the beginning.

Sam Wanamaker was the founder of the modern Globe Theatre **House** which	....House....	0
was built near the original site on the South Bank of the River Thames.	✓	00
His idea to rebuild the Globe goes back then to his first visit to London in 1949.	....	Q1
At the time he wanted to visit the historic site. But what he found out was	....	Q2
only a plaque on a building referring to the Globe. The idea to revive	....	Q3
this famous theatre production was to occupy him for rest of his life.	....	Q4
In 1970 he had founded the Shakespeare Globe Trust whose main	....	Q5
function was to procure money pockets for the reconstruction of the original	....	Q6
theatre and to coordinate research efforts to make sure that the replica	....	Q7
of the Globe was to be as close to the original as even possible.	....	Q8

6 Language in use: Being a literary critic is not easy

You are going to read a text about the job of a literary critic. Some words are missing from the text. Choose the correct answer (A, B, C or D) for each gap (1–13) in the text. Write your answers in the boxes provided. The first one (0) has been done for you.

Literary … **(0)** are a very distinct group of people. What we enjoy as … **(Q1)** is part of their job. … **(Q2)** of getting carried away by a performance they have to watch and analyse at the same time. On … **(Q3)** of that they also have to remember and to take … **(Q4)** of what they have seen and which thoughts have gone through their minds. However, in most cases they will have read the text … **(Q5)**, but occasionally that may not be possible, especially when they have to write a review of a … **(Q6)** play.

   One of the difficulties is that they are not supposed to only provide a … **(Q7)** of the play and character descriptions but also an analysis of the performance itself. This includes a … **(Q8)** of the way in which the play was put on stage, a comment on the actors and their individual performances, an analysis of the work of the director, who usually has a … **(Q9)** influence on how a play is received by the audience, and much more.

   In the … **(Q10)** of William Shakespeare literary critics also need to know a lot about Shakespeare's time, the conditions under which plays were produced back then and ideally they should have studied the latest … **(Q11)** on the most famous author of the English language.

   And if you start having your doubts about present-day literary critics, you may be right. But this is not necessarily their … **(Q12)** but rather due to the nature of their … **(Q13)** job.

0	A	critique	B	critical	C	critics	D	criticism
Q1	A	public	B	spectators	C	visitor	D	auditorium
Q2	A	For	B	Because	C	Instead	D	Close
Q3	A	grounds	B	idea	C	height	D	top
Q4	A	notes	B	notices	C	notifications	D	noteworthy
Q5	A	alone	B	towards	C	after	D	beforehand
Q6	A	actual	B	contemporary	C	topical	D	current
Q7	A	view	B	summary	C	part	D	story
Q8	A	criticism	B	critic	C	review	D	criticaster
Q9	A	considering	B	considerable	C	considerate	D	considered
Q10	A	fall	B	domain	C	strand	D	case
Q11	A	research	B	foundations	C	finds	D	fines
Q12	A	fault	B	guilt	C	problem	D	mangel
Q13	A	demanded	B	deceiving	C	decisive	D	demanding

0	Q1	Q2	Q3	Q4	Q5	Q6	Q7	Q8	Q9	Q10	Q11	Q12	Q13
C													

Prime Time 8

Ireland

1 Finding the right meaning

Match the words on the left with the correct definitions or examples on the right.

1. clash	K	**A**	to create sound by blowing air through one's lips
2. to suspend		**B**	to drive out
3. famine		**C**	to give up
4. to defeat		**D**	hunger, period of extreme food shortage
5. to suppress		**E**	long narrow box used to bury people
6. to surrender		**F**	to officially prevent sb. from holding office
7. to oust		**G**	organised like a regular army
8. poverty		**H**	Protestant clergyman
9. coffin		**I**	to put an end to sth. with force
10. to whistle		**J**	state of being poor
11. paramilitary		**K**	violent confrontation
12. reverend		**L**	to win a victory over

2 Language in use: Irish literature

You are going to read a text about Irish literature. Some words are missing from the text. Fill in the word which best fits each gap (1–8). Use only one word in each gap. Write your answers in the spaces provided at the end of the text. The first one (0) has been done for you.

Ireland is a comparatively … **(0)** country but it has made a disproportionate contribution to the world of literature. The … **(Q1)** best known around the world are written in English, but Gaelic, the Celtic language of Ireland, also has a significant body of literature going back to … **(Q2)** times. The two strands of Irish literature are a consequence of the political situation as Ireland was … **(Q3)** from England for many centuries. Irish literature … **(Q4)** from other literary traditions as Irish … **(Q5)** have a very special sense of wonder in the face of nature and a narrative style which tends to be exaggerated and sometimes satirical.

Some of the greatest authors of the English language were Irish. Novelists such as James Joyce, a Dublin-born … **(Q6)**, who struggled with his concept of Ireland for his whole life, are well-known for their literary works. Dramatists like George Bernard Shaw are equally … **(Q7)** and have left their mark on world literature. The long-standing Irish story-telling … **(Q8)** seems to be the foundation of the literary influence of the country.

0	small	✔

Q1 ....

Q2 ....

Q3 ....

Q4 ....

Q5 ....

Q6 ....

Q7 ....

Q8 ....

3 Rephrasing: Events in Irish history

Rewrite the following text passages with the words given. Compare your answers with the sample answers in the key.

1. 12th century: First incursions by England; Ulster (northern part of island) conquered in 1177

   to attack/to invade – to take full control

   In the 12th century England first attacked/ .... invaded Ulster, the northern part of the island, ... before it took full control in 1177. ....

2. 17th century: Start of "Plantation of Ulster", systematic colonisation of the northern part of the island by settlers from England and Scotland; after English Civil War Cromwell conquers whole of Ireland

   to form – to colonise – English forces – to occupy

   ....
   ....
   ....
   ....
   ....

3. 1690: Protestant King William of Orange defeats deposed King James at Battle of the Boyne; confirms claim to English throne and Ireland

   to beat – to oust – to strengthen one's hold of

   ....
   ....
   ....
   ....
   ....

4. 1800: Parliamentary Union of Ireland and Britain

   to form

   ....
   ....
   ....
   ....
   ....

5. 1916: The "Easter Rising", uprising in Dublin against British rule; defeat and execution of leaders

   to stage – to suppress – to surrender – to sentence to death – to shoot

   ....
   ....
   ....
   ....
   ....

4 Plural forms

a) Write the plural forms into the correct boxes below.

> ~~analysis~~ • ~~bacterium~~ • basis • ~~box~~ • bush • ~~calf~~ • ~~child~~ • class • ~~craft~~ • crisis •
> ~~criterion~~ • curriculum • deer • fish • ~~foot~~ • fox • goose • half • ~~headquarters~~ • ~~hero~~ •
> ~~journey~~ • key • knife • leaf • life • ~~louse~~ • man • match • means • medium •
> mouse • offspring • ox • phenomenon • potato • -self • series • sheep • shelf •
> species • thesis • thief • tomato • tooth • volcano • wolf • woman

-is → -es	-o → -es	... → -es
analyses	heroes	boxes

-f(e) → -ves	-ey → -eys	-oo- → -ee-
calves	journeys	feet

-on → -a	-um → -a	-ouse → -ice
criteria	bacteria	lice

Complete change	No change (singular)	No change (plural)
children	craft	headquarters

b) Look up the words you don't know in an online dictionary, check the meaning and write one sample phrase or sentence in your exercise book.

5 Language in use: The Queen and the IRA commander

You are going to read a text about a historic state visit of the Irish President to Windsor Castle. Some words are missing from the text. Choose the correct answer (A, B, C or D) for each gap (1–12) in the text. Write your answers in the boxes provided. The first one (0) has been done for you.

10 April 2014 marked a new era … **(0)** Anglo-Irish relations when former IRA commander Martin McGuinness shook hands … **(Q1)** the Queen at Windsor Castle … **(Q2)** the occasion of a state visit by the Irish President. The event was held to recognise the contribution of British and Irish individuals who have furthered co-operation, enterprise and culture between Britain and Northern Ireland.

The Queen and the Duke of Edinburgh greeted and chatted to the guests, who included MPs and MEPs (Members of the European Parliament) … **(Q3)** Northern Ireland, and medal-winning Olympic and Paralympic athletes. Mr McGuinness shook hands with the Queen and congratulated her … **(Q4)** her role in peace-making in Ireland.

He said, "The Queen's visit … **(Q5)** Dublin and how she conducted herself – her words … **(Q6)** the memorial in Dublin and how she reached out to all victims without differentiating – were all hugely impressive. She had many reasons not to meet me, and me her, but I think we've risen above that and seen the contribution that these big acts … **(Q7)** reconciliation can have. I'm overjoyed … **(Q8)** the president. He is my president and I'm delighted he's been given such a great welcome."

However, this event did not go by … **(Q9)** protests of victims of the conflict in Northern Ireland. But in spite of all this the Irish state visit to Windsor marked an important step in the UK and Irish relations.

Ireland's Foreign Affairs Minister, Eamon Gilmore, said that Ireland and the UK had reached a "new platform" which meant an enormous amount … **(Q10)** all the Irish living in Britain, who had memories … **(Q11)** difficult times. That visit was an event loaded … **(Q12)** symbolism all the way through, but the general sentiment was that the visit was memorable, uplifting and positive.

(Tara Brady, *Daily Mail*, 10 April 2014; adapted and abridged)

0	A	on	B	for	C̶	in	D	from
Q1	A	to	B	with	C	on	D	upon
Q2	A	for	B	from	C	on	D	to
Q3	A	from	B	among	C	between	D	in
Q4	A	at	B	on	C	for	D	onto
Q5	A	at	B	in	C	for	D	to
Q6	A	on	B	at	C	in	D	under
Q7	A	for	B	of	C	in	D	on
Q8	A	for	B	to	C	at	D	during
Q9	A	with	B	without	C	for	D	of
Q10	A	on	B	from	C	to	D	among
Q11	A	at	B	for	C	with	D	of
Q12	A	to	B	on	C	in	D	with

0	Q1	Q2	Q3	Q4	Q5	Q6	Q7	Q8	Q9	Q10	Q11	Q12
C ✓												

6 Language in use: Saint Patrick's Day

You are going to read a text about Saint Patrick's Day. Some words are missing from the text. Choose from the list (A–P) the correct part for each gap (1–13) in the text. There are two extra words you should not use. Write your answers in the boxes provided. The first one (0) has been done for you.

In America, Saint Patrick's Day, on 17 March, has long been commemorated with lively … **(0)**, but until recent decades, the holiday, which honours Ireland's patron saint, was traditionally a more solemn occasion on the Emerald Isle.

The man for whom Saint Patrick's Day is named was born into an aristocratic … **(Q1)** in Roman Britain around the end of the fourth century. As a teenager, he was kidnapped by Irish … **(Q2)** and taken to Ireland, where he was held as a slave for a number of years. He eventually … **(Q3)** from the island, only to return later as a missionary and … **(Q4)** part of the population to Christianity. Centuries after his death, which some sources cite as 17 March 461, although the exact date is unknown, Patrick became the patron saint of Ireland, and 17 March became a holy day of obligation for the nation's Catholics.

Thanks to Irish … **(Q5)** in the United States and elsewhere, Saint Patrick's Day evolved from a religious … **(Q6)** into a secular celebration of all things Irish. The first Saint Patrick's Day … **(Q7)** was held in New York City in the 1760s, by Irishmen serving there in the British military. During the 19th century, when Irish Catholic immigrants faced … **(Q8)** in Protestant-majority America, Saint Patrick's Day parades became an … **(Q9)** to show strength in numbers. Today, with some 34.5 million Americans claiming to be primarily or partially of Irish … **(Q10)** – making Irish ancestry the second-most commonly reported in the United States, after German – the tradition of wearing green on 17 March is still going strong. Australia and Canada are among other countries with long-standing Saint Paddy's Day traditions.

Meanwhile, back in the old country, where until the 1970s pubs were closed on Saint Patrick's Day, the Irish are … **(Q11)** with their counterparts across the ocean when it comes to revelry. Since the mid-1990s, the government, in part to promote tourism and … **(Q12)** the economy, has sponsored a multi-day Saint Patrick's Festival in Dublin, featuring a parade and a variety of performances and activities; there are similar … **(Q13)** in other sections of the country as well.

(*History.com*, 17 March 2014; adapted and abridged)

A	backpackers	**H**	escaped	**O**	parade	**0**	K ✓
B	boost	**I**	events	**P**	pirates	**Q1**	
C	catching up	**J**	family			**Q2**	
D	converse	**K**	festivities			**Q3**	
E	convert	**L**	holiday			**Q4**	
F	descent	**M**	immigrants			**Q5**	
G	discrimination	**N**	opportunity			**Q6**	

Q7			
Q8			
Q9			
Q10			
Q11			
Q12			
Q13			

Saving the planet

1 Climate change

a) Write down a definition for each of the words below, combining one phrase from column 1 and one phrase from column 2. Make sure that you use the right forms and tenses.

1. biofuel **2.** carbon dioxide (CO_2) **3.** carbon footprint **4.** climate change

5. deforestation **6.** fossil fuels **7.** global warming **8.** greenhouse effect

9. mitigation **10.** renewable energy **11.** weather

Column 1	Column 2
fuel derived from renewable, biological sources	produce carbon dioxide when burned
pattern of change affecting the global or regional climate	including crops such as maize and sugar cane
insulating effect of certain gases in the atmosphere	by-product of human activities such as burning fossil fuels
formed in the Earth over millions of years	such as average temperature and rainfall
principal greenhouse gas produced by human activity	allows solar radiation to warm the earth
state of the atmosphere	in a given period of time
amount of carbon emitted by an individual or organisation	with regard to temperature, cloudiness, rainfall, wind and other meteorological conditions
permanent removal of standing forests	by reducing greenhouse gas emissions or absorbing greenhouse gases in the atmosphere
energy created from sources that can be replenished in a short period of time	largely caused by man-made greenhouse gas emissions
action that will reduce man-made climate change	leading to significant levels of carbon dioxide emissions
steady rise in global average temperature	biomass, the movement of water, geothermal, wind, and solar

b) Complete the sentences with suitable words from above.

1. The United Nations warn that growing crops to make "green" .... *biofuel* .... drives up food prices.
2. A new app lets you tie your .... with what you buy.
3. Their fumes contributed to the .... which causes the polar ice caps to melt.
4. A combination of climate change and .... is making the Amazon rainforest increasingly vulnerable to devastating forest fires.
5. Much of the air pollution is caused by burning .... to generate heat and electricity.
6. .... with the exception of offshore wind power is getting cheaper all the time.
7. The region can experience extreme .... that can include high winds and heavy rains.
8. The operation will contribute to climate change .... by using renewable energy sources and energy efficiency enhancements.

2 Language in use: Severn Suzuki's speech at the UN Earth Summit

a) You are going to read the full text of Severn Suzuki's speech at the UN Earth Summit. Some words are missing from the text. Choose the correct answer (A, B, C or D) for each gap (1–12) in the text. Write your answers in the boxes provided. The first one (0) has been done for you.

Hello, I'm Severn Suzuki speaking for ECO, The Environmental Children's Organisation. We are a group of twelve- and thirteen-year-olds trying to make a difference: Vanessa Suttie, Morgan Geisler, Michelle Quigg and me. We … **(0)** all the money to come here ourselves, to come five thousand miles to tell you adults you must change your ways.

Coming here today, I have no hidden … **(Q1)**. I am fighting for my future. Losing my future is not like losing an election or a few points on the stock market. I am here to speak for all generations to come. I am here to speak on … **(Q2)** of the starving children around the world whose cries go unheard. I am here to speak for the countless animals dying across this planet because they have nowhere left to go. I am afraid to go out in the sun now because of the holes in our ozone layer. I am afraid to breathe the air because I don't know what chemicals are in it.

I used to go fishing in Vancouver, my home, with my dad until just a few years ago we found the fish full of cancers. And now we hear of animals and plants going … **(Q3)** every day – vanishing forever. In my life, I have dreamt of seeing the great herds of wild animals, jungles and rainforests full of birds and butterflies, but now I wonder if they will even exist for my children to see. Did you have to worry about these little things when you were my age?

All this is happening before our eyes and yet we act as if we have all the time we want and all the solutions. I'm only a child and I don't have all the solutions, but I want you to realise, … **(Q4)** do you! You don't know how to fix the holes in our ozone layer. You don't know how to bring the salmon back up a dead stream. You don't know how to bring back an

animal now extinct. And you can't bring back the forest that once grew where there is now desert. If you don't know how to fix it, please stop breaking it!

Here, you may be … **(Q5)** of your governments, business people, organisers, reporters or politicians, but really you are mothers and fathers, sisters and brothers, aunts and uncles. And all of you are someone's child. I'm only a child, yet I know we are all part of a family, five billion strong; in fact, 30 million species strong, and we all … **(Q6)** the same air, water and soil – borders and governments will never change that. I'm only a child, yet I know we are all in this together and should act as one single world … **(Q7)** one single goal. In my anger, I am not blind, and in my fear, I am not afraid of telling the world how I feel.

In my country, we make so much waste, we buy and throw away, buy and throw away, and yet northern countries will not share with the needy. Even when we have more than enough, we are afraid to share. We are afraid to let go of some of our wealth. In Canada, we live the … **(Q8)** life, with plenty of food, water and shelter. We have watches, bicycles, computers and television sets. The list could go on for two days.

Two days ago here in Brazil, we were shocked when we spent some time with some children living on the streets. This is what one child told us, "I wish I was rich. And if I were, I would give all the street children food, clothes, medicine, shelter and love and affection." If a child on the street who has nothing is willing to share, why are we who have everything still so greedy? I can't stop thinking that these are children my own age, that it makes a tremendous … **(Q9)** where you are born, that I could be one of those children living in the Favelas of Rio. I could be a child starving in Somalia, or a victim of war in the Middle East, or a beggar in India.

I'm only a child, yet I know if all the money spent on war was spent on finding environmental answers, ending poverty and finding treaties, what a wonderful place this earth would be! At school, even in kindergarten, you teach us to behave in the world. You teach us: not to fight with others, to … (Q10) things out, to respect others, to clean up our mess, not to hurt other creatures, to share and not be greedy. Then why do you go out and do the things you tell us not to do?

Do not forget why you're attending these conferences, who you're doing this for: We are your own children. You are deciding what kind of world we will grow up in. Parents should be able to … (Q11) their children by saying "everything's going to be alright", "it's not the end of the world" and "we're doing the best we can". But I don't think you can say that to us anymore. Are we even on your list of priorities?

My dad always says, "You are what you do, not what you say." Well, what you do makes me cry at night. You grownups say you love us. But I challenge you: Please make your actions … (Q12) your words. Thank you for listening.

0	A	raised	B	brought	C	took	D	asked
Q1	A	agenda	B	image	C	calendar	D	record
Q2	A	side	B	benefit	C	behalf	D	representation
Q3	A	alive	B	extinct	C	departed	D	dead
Q4	A	either	B	nor	C	neither	D	or
Q5	A	agents	B	replacements	C	regents	D	delegates
Q6	A	claim	B	divide	C	serve	D	share
Q7	A	until	B	towards	C	before	D	against
Q8	A	honoured	B	superior	C	privileged	D	disadvantageous
Q9	A	contrast	B	regularity	C	change	D	difference
Q10	A	work	B	make	C	ask	D	plan
Q11	A	comfort	B	favour	C	please	D	upset
Q12	A	reverse	B	reply	C	request	D	reflect

0	Q1	Q2	Q3	Q4	Q5	Q6	Q7	Q8	Q9	Q10	Q11	Q12
A ✓												

b) Complete the following sentences with passages from Severn Suzuki's speech.

We have to see to it that … .	
We should take care not to … .	
We need to adopt a resolution to … .	
Our most pressing problem is … .	
We have to negotiate an agreement to … .	
We are hopeful/confident that … .	
We are working to … .	

3 Building a sustainable food source

Complete the following text on the question how we will feed the planet in 2050 with the correct forms of the verbs given.

If you have any lingering illusions that your weekly grocery shop ....*is going to decrease*........ (**1 decrease**) in cost miraculously, forget about them. Rising food prices are a reality we .... (**2 have to**) deal with in future.

"The era of cheap food is over," says sustainable food expert Paul McMahon. He explains, "There are solid reasons to believe food .... (**3 stay**) more expensive in the next decades because of severe weather conditions around the globe and the production of biofuels. We .... (**4 see**) higher food prices than before."

McMahon is adamant that the planet .... (**5 not run out**) of food, but that issues with overproduction and distribution are preventing it from getting to everyone. "Fundamentally, people go hungry not because there isn't enough food but because they can't afford to buy food," he says. "To address that problem, we .... (**6 need**) to help poorer communities earn higher incomes and go through a process of economic development."

Times had changed from the 1980s, when there were regular media reports about "butter mountains" and "wine lakes" across Europe. "Because food has been too cheap, we have taken it for granted," McMahon explains. "As food .... (**7 get**) more expensive, one of the positive benefits of that probably .... (**8 be**) that we waste less because we .... (**9 think**) more carefully about what we buy and make sure that less ends up in the bin."

"The real problem is underproduction in poor countries," McMahon analyses. "The advice which a lot of those countries were given for many years was: Don't worry about growing your own food because you can always rely on cheap American or European exports. That turned out not to be a good strategy for food security or economic development." According to the expert, it's necessary that in the future small farmers in Africa in particular .... (**10 empower**) to grow more for their domestic markets so that eventually these regions .... (**11 become**) a bread basket for the rest of the world too because of the big reserves of land and water.

For now, it looks as if the increase in food prices .... (**12 continue**). "There are some fundamental supply-and-demand reasons why prices are high," says McMahon. "Total world production of the basic grains wheat, rice and maize was lower than world consumption for seven out of eight years. We are, in effect, living off our reserves. It's inevitable you .... (**13 have**) high prices in that situation when you have tight supplies. The high price is not the problem in itself – it's a symptom of those underlying problems."

(Ross McGuiness, *Metro.co.uk*, 3 April 2013; adapted and abridged)

4 "Passive houses" vs. "Active houses"

Houses are stationary objects, so using terms like "passive" and "active" to describe them initially seems a little odd. These terms actually refer to design strategies that create comfort for occupants while drastically cutting down on energy use.

Passive strategies take advantage of nature – specifically the sun and wind – to achieve comfort. This approach builds on traditional methods that have been used in residential design for centuries. Active houses follow passive design techniques but take them to the next level by producing their own energy.

a) *Passive houses and active houses possess certain distinguishing features. First, have a look at the keywords below and fill in the suitable words into the gaps in the middle column.*

absorb   climates   expensive   insulated   loss   low

moisture   ~~site~~   stale   windows

Category	"Passive" housing	"Active" housing
location	..........*site*.......... **(1)** orientation: a home should be positioned to take advantage of the path of the sun	
building materials	properly .... **(2)** walls and roofs that .... **(3)** heat from the sun and warm the house at night	
	triple-pane .... **(4)** to prevent heat .... **(5)** or gain	
technology	heat-recovery system exchanges .... **(6)** for fresh air and eliminates mould-causing .... **(7)**	
	quite .... **(8)**-tech: no need for air conditioner or furnace	*quite high-tech: computer system regulates, monitors, and adjusts power use*
costs	approximately 10% more .... **(9)** to construct than conventional house	
possible problems	strategies might not work in all .... **(10)**	

 b) *Go online and find out which features apply to active houses. Write them into the right-hand column.*

c) *Write sentences that contrast the two ideas. Use words and phrases from below.*

> although • as a consequence • as well as • besides • even though •
> for this reason • furthermore • however • in addition • in spite of •
> moreover • nevertheless • not only … but also • on the contrary •
> on the one hand … on the other hand • therefore • whereas

Gender issues

1 Finding the right meaning

a) *Match the boxes that have the same meaning. Each pair consists of an odd (e.g. 1, 3, 5, …) and an even number (2, 4, 6, …).*

1 prejudice	2 prolonged public disagreement or heated discussion	3 to be domesticated	4 when a man marries a man or a woman a woman	5 suffrage movement
6 the same chances	7 to be on a par with sth./sb.	8 slow process of change	9 intolerable	10 to be focused on one's success
11 controversy	12 educating boys and girls separately	13 majority	14 to be tamed	15 equal opportunities
16 unacceptable	17 to be career-oriented	18 bias	19 trend	20 to be obsolete
21 disparity	22 people fighting for the right to vote	23 same-sex marriage	24 tendency	25 single-sex education
26 the greater number	27 to be a thing of the past	28 great difference	29 gradual development	30 equal in importance or quality to

Odd numbers	1	3	5	7	9	11	13	15	17	19	21	23	25	27	29
Even numbers	18														

b) *Look up the words you don't know.*

c) *Use each word or phrase in a sentence.*

2 How to speculate

*a) Match the words or phrases below with the ones in **bold print**. Use the correct forms.*

to figure out   to guess   to read between lines   ~~to reflect on~~

to review   to suspect   to wonder

1. He **thought about** his behaviour and then he decided that he had to be more careful in the way he talked to people.
reflected on ....

2. My mum bought a book about gender differences because she wanted to **write about** it in our local paper.
....

3. When I asked her about it I had to **guess what she meant** because she was very vague about it.
....

4. I had no clue what the correct answer was, so I had to **choose one that appealed to me**.
....

5. It was hard to **understand** why the numbers had dropped dramatically.
....

6. The detective **had a feeling** that the murderer was still in the area.
....

7. None of the waiters paid any attention to us, so we **asked ourselves** whether we should stay or leave.
....

b) Match the sentences with the most appropriate words or phrases.

1. to brainstorm	D	A	She has started to **focus on her thoughts** in order to relieve some of her stress from work.
2. to build castles in the air		B	When he found out more about his father's upbringing, he had to **think about** his life **carefully** the whole afternoon.
3. to ponder		C	Instead of working on her paper Clare spends most of her time **daydreaming**.
4. to consider		D	They thought about the problem carefully and tried to solve it by **looking for** various options.
5. to deliberate on		E	If they had really cared for him, Michael **thought logically**, they would have stayed.
6. to meditate		F	There are quite a few things to **think about** before we can decide what to do next.
7. to reason		G	The group of conspirators **planned** to overthrow the government.
8. to scheme		H	In the end I **think** she will get everything, which is what she wanted all along.
9. to suppose		I	Ida **thought about** how to start her talk at the conference **for a long time**, and then suddenly rose and left.

c) Rewrite the sentences from tasks a and b with the alternative words and phrases in the correct form.

3 Language in use: I do not want to give up "me"

You are going to read a text about the challenges of motherhood. Some forms are missing from the text. Choose from the list (A–P) the correct part for each gap (1–13) in the text. There are two extra forms you should not use. Write your answers in the boxes provided. The first one (0) has been done for you.

I am a mother, currently … **(0)** with my second child. I had my daughter while working in New York and got eleven weeks paid leave, after which I voluntarily … **(Q1)** to work. This time round I'm taking six months. It feels like a luxury to have that … **(Q2)** with my son, but I am looking forward to … **(Q3)** to work.

Raising children is very hard work. But I do not believe that I have to do it … **(Q4)**. Neither does my husband. We chose to have our family; it is our responsibility to work for it. There's an African proverb that says it … **(Q5)** a village to raise a child. Nowadays the "village" consists of professional day care that nurtures, entertains and teaches, … **(Q6)** family and friends and kids clubs. I truly believe that these and all the other "village" options are good things, both for my children, my family … **(Q7)** and for me.

I have studied and worked long and hard to … **(Q8)** where I am. I am good at my job and … **(Q9)** from it. I am happy to acknowledge that I couldn't stay at home … **(Q10)** with my children long term. I crave a different kind of stimulation. I do not want to … **(Q11)** "me". If I was resentful of giving up "me", my children would feel it. And whilst my focus has now changed, it does not mean that I cannot … **(Q12)** both work and motherhood.

I think we fixate too much on the idea of perfection – and how someone must have it "right". If you want to work, work. If you want to stay at home, stay at home. If you want to stay at home but have to work – I hope you can … **(Q13)** of the situation.

(Nicki Leaper, The Guardian, 13 April 2012)

A	all day long	**H**	get pleasure	**O**	returned	**0**	M ✓	**Q7**
B	all myself	**I**	get to	**P**	takes	**Q1**		**Q8**
C	amount of time	**J**	give up			**Q2**		**Q9**
D	as a whole	**K**	going back			**Q3**		**Q10**
E	combine	**L**	make the best			**Q4**		**Q11**
F	consider	**M**	make up for			**Q5**		**Q12**
G	extended	**N**	on maternity leave			**Q6**		**Q13**

4 Vocabulary: Living with children

a) Study the text from the previous task and make a list of words and phrases related to family life with young children. Use this list when you have to talk or write about this topic.

on maternity leave
…

b) Go online, find more words and phrases related to this topic and collect them in your exercise book.

5 Are single women discriminated against at work?

Read through the text below and underline all the expressions that have something to do with the world of work and with women and their role in the workplace.

Your co-worker with a three-year-old leaves at 5:30 every evening, while you stay until 7:30 (at least). You're asked to take a weekend shift or deal with Saturday conference calls because
5 everyone else on your team has kids they need to spend time with. When an issue needs to be sorted out after six, you are somehow always the only one available, and it's made clear that your date plans are not a priority.
10 If this sounds like you, you may be the victim of what a recent *Marie Claire* article calls "the newest form of workplace discrimination: Single women who carry an unfair burden at the office, and stand in for their married-with-
15 kids co-workers."
Employers have got used to working parents leaving at a reasonable hour and not working weekends, they've also got used to single staffers, particularly single women, picking up the work that employees with kids won't get to. 20 The result for those single women is no personal life, which limits both their overall well-being and their ability to meet a prospective partner and have children of their own.
Even if single men face the same dilemma, 25 it's easy to see how single women are especially vulnerable to it. The most popular job for American women as of 2010 is still secretary/administrative assistant, which has been a top ten job for women for the last 50 years. We're 30 historically conditioned to think of female workers as those who support other workers. At the same time, women have just been told to be as ambitious as they can, which can very easily translate into saying "yes" to whatever 35 project is handed to them.

(Margaret Wheeler Johnson, *The Huffington Post*, 26 June 2013; adapted and abridged)

6 Language in use: Female authors who use male pseudonyms

You are going to read a text about female authors and their choice of pseudonyms. In most lines of the text there is a word that should not be there. Write that word in the space provided after each line. Some lines are correct. Indicate these lines with a tick (✓). There are two examples at the beginning.

The use of pseudonyms by writers is as **super** rich and varied as the history	......*super*...... **0**
of literature itself. Every author has his or her own reason for publishing	......✓...... **00**
certain works under a pen friend name. Some authors want to branch out	.... **Q1**
into other genres without of risking their reputations in an attempt to	.... **Q2**
explore a new writing voice over with minimal consequence. However, the	.... **Q3**
adoption of pen names is not always the author's choice. There was a time	.... **Q4**
when female writers were led to believe in that their gender prevented their	.... **Q5**
works from being taken seriously modern. Though women have made great	.... **Q6**
strides in literature, that same out-dated belief continues to affect women	.... **Q7**
writers. Perhaps recognising some out of the more famous writers who	.... **Q8**
found no success after leaving their male pseudonyms behind will show	.... **Q9**
that a woman doesn't need a man's name to set the literary world ablaze.	.... **Q10**
One last example is J.K. Rowling, who was told by her publisher that her series	.... **Q11**
wouldn't be as popular among boys if it was published under the name of a	.... **Q12**
woman. So she used to a set of initials instead (not even her own, since she	.... **Q13**
has no first middle name) and, as we all know, the Harry Potter books	.... **Q14**
catapulted in popularity even after her gender role was revealed.	.... **Q15**
What would the world of literature be like without the contributions of these	.... **Q16**
women? It is not very sad that, despite all of the achievements of female	.... **Q17**
writers, a novel's commercial success is still connected to its author's gender –	.... **Q18**
at least in the black eyes of publishers.	.... **Q19**

7 English similes

a) Form typical English similes.

1.	as big as	I	A	a bat	7.	as cold as		G	a lord
2.	as black as		B	a bee	8.	as cunning as		H	a pancake
3.	as blind as		C	a bird	9.	as dead as		I	an elephant
4.	as brave as		D	a doornail	10.	as drunk as		J	coal
5.	as busy as		E	a fox	11.	as flat as		K	crystal
6.	as clear as		F	a lion	12.	as free as		L	ice

b) Complete the following sentences with words or phrases from the box.

> a church mouse • a ghost • ~~a lamb~~ • a dog •
> a razor • a wolf • gold • life • silk • the hills

1. Our new Spanish teacher is as gentle as ………*a lamb*………, even though most people are cautious when meeting her.

2. As soon as I had told them I had to leave, they were as good as ……………………………………………… .

3. Steve hadn't packed enough food for his hike, so when he returned to the camp in the evening he was as hungry as ……………………………………………… .

4. Here they were, as large as ……………………………………………… – Graham with his long hair and Ian with his Northern accent.

5. An adult can seem both ageless and as old as ……………………………………………… to a child.

6. My great-grandfather worked day in and day out, but in spite of all his efforts he remained as poor as ……………………………………………… .

7. Marie Curie's mind was as sharp as ……………………………………………… .

8. When the boat started rolling I was as sick as ……………………………………………… .

9. But only half an hour later the water was as smooth as ……………………………………………… .

10. When he came out of the operating theatre he was as white as ……………………………………………… .

c) Combine adjectives and nouns from the table and write down similes.

~~stubborn~~	an eel	sturdy	the grave	tall	lightning	timid
a snail	wise	a rock	white	an arrow	tough	an ox
quick	a giraffe	silent	an oak	slippery	~~a mule~~	slow
a mouse	strong	old boots	straight	snow	solid	an owl

as stubborn as a mule, …

Migration

1 Analysing statistics

a) *Study the graph and the historical details below. Take a text marker and highlight the important years in the graph so that you can refer to them later.*

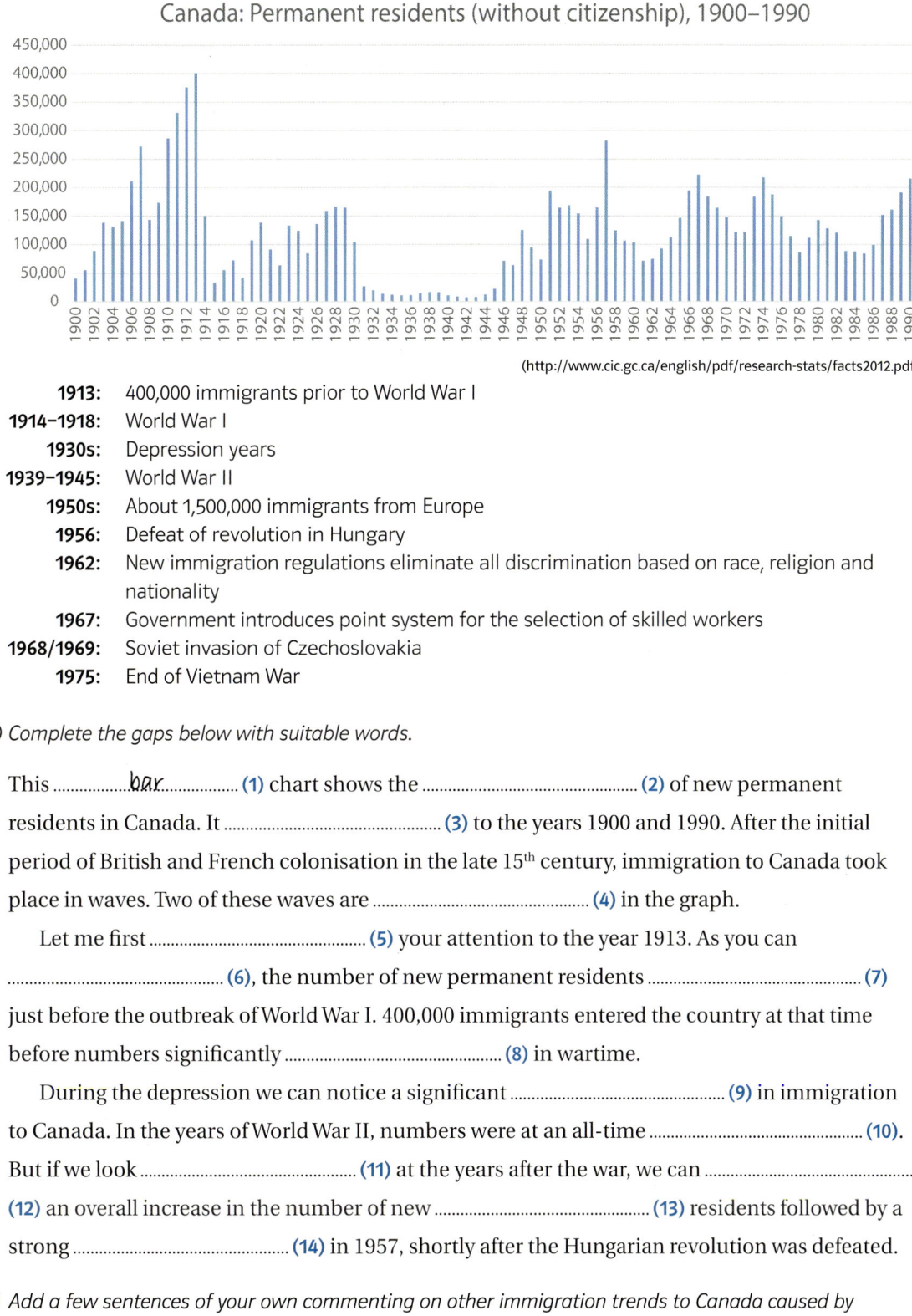

Canada: Permanent residents (without citizenship), 1900–1990

(http://www.cic.gc.ca/english/pdf/research-stats/facts2012.pdf)

1913:	400,000 immigrants prior to World War I
1914–1918:	World War I
1930s:	Depression years
1939–1945:	World War II
1950s:	About 1,500,000 immigrants from Europe
1956:	Defeat of revolution in Hungary
1962:	New immigration regulations eliminate all discrimination based on race, religion and nationality
1967:	Government introduces point system for the selection of skilled workers
1968/1969:	Soviet invasion of Czechoslovakia
1975:	End of Vietnam War

b) *Complete the gaps below with suitable words.*

This ....bar............ **(1)** chart shows the .... **(2)** of new permanent residents in Canada. It .... **(3)** to the years 1900 and 1990. After the initial period of British and French colonisation in the late 15ᵗʰ century, immigration to Canada took place in waves. Two of these waves are .... **(4)** in the graph.

Let me first .... **(5)** your attention to the year 1913. As you can .... **(6)**, the number of new permanent residents .... **(7)** just before the outbreak of World War I. 400,000 immigrants entered the country at that time before numbers significantly .... **(8)** in wartime.

During the depression we can notice a significant .... **(9)** in immigration to Canada. In the years of World War II, numbers were at an all-time .... **(10)**. But if we look .... **(11)** at the years after the war, we can .... **(12)** an overall increase in the number of new .... **(13)** residents followed by a strong .... **(14)** in 1957, shortly after the Hungarian revolution was defeated.

c) *Add a few sentences of your own commenting on other immigration trends to Canada caused by certain historical events.*

2 Word formation: The story of Filipino immigration to Canada

a) Fill the gaps in the table with the appropriate word. Use a dictionary if you need help.

Verb	Noun (person)	Noun	Adjective
to achieve			*achievable*
		arrival	
to connect			
		dedication	
			electable
	facilitator		
–	–	immediacy	
to immigrate			
	–	integration	
	nurse		
–	–		permanent
		residency	
to settle			
			sponsored
	–	strengthening	

b) Complete the sentences with suitable words from above.

1. The ....**strengthening**....... of the recovery from the Great Recession in the advanced economies is a positive development.

2. Future tenants need to pass a so-called .... test before being allowed into a social home.

3. A rescued falcon has been released into the wild after being .... back to health.

4. The Duchess and Duke have been greeted with wild applause by thousands of people on their .... at the Sydney Opera House.

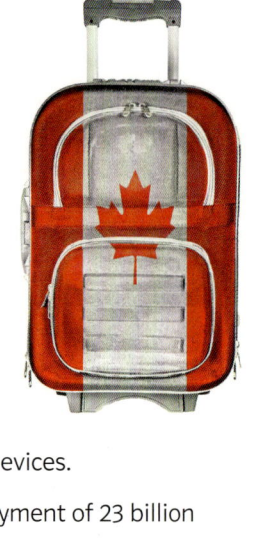

5. It can act as an audio and charging dock for USB-... devices.

6. An independent Scotland would face an .... debt repayment of 23 billion pounds to the UK Treasury.

7. With a special dog menu, luxury beds and even access to a spa, this London hotel is taking its .... to man's best friend seriously.

8. In the next primary .... voters will find several changes in the voting process.

9. One loud rock concert or sporting event could cause .... hearing damage.

10. Choose an .... time frame to accomplish your goals.

c) *You are going to read a text on immigration to Canada. Some words are missing from the text. Use the words in brackets to complete each gap (1–14) in the text. Write your answers in the spaces provided at the end of the text. The first one (0) has been done for you.*

In just a few decades, Canada's Filipino community has grown from less than a thousand residents to one of the country's largest … **(0 immigrate)** demographics. At present, over 500,000 Filipinos call Canada their home, and this number is increasing rapidly. In fact, in recent years the Philippines has been the greatest source of immigrants to Canada.

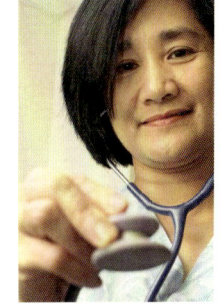

The story of Filipino immigration to Canada is one of dreams, hard work, sacrifice and success. In 2012 alone, over 32,000 new Canadian permanent … **(Q1 reside)** came to Canada from the Philippines – a massive 146 per cent increase from 2004. Many new … **(Q2 arrive)** came to work as live-in caregivers across Canada, especially in major Canadian metropolises like Toronto. Today, over 200,000 Filipino immigrants reside in the greater Toronto area, more than in any other city.

Many Filipinos have worked hard to bring their … **(Q3 immediacy)** families to Canada. Many people who came to Canada as temporary workers left spouses and children behind. Once … **(Q4 permanency)** residency was … **(Q5 achievement)**, they were then able to reunite with their families in Canada. Canada's family … **(Q6 sponsor)** rules allow permanent residents to sponsor not only children and spouses, but parents and grandparents as well.

Whether from the Philippines or any other country, there is no "typical" immigrant to Canada. Filipinos in Canada work in a wide range of disciplines in every province in the country. Because many Filipinos have a good command of the English language, they are able to find jobs and quickly … **(Q7 settlement)** into their new homes upon arrival. Many Filipino immigrants find work in one of two popular fields: … **(Q8 nurse)** and caregiving. Prospective immigrants with experience in these fields are in luck, as Canada has many immigration programmes geared towards workers with these skill sets. Canada has a … **(Q9 dedicate)** Live-In Caregiver Programme that … **(Q10 facilitation)** the entry of these workers to the country. In addition, popular immigration programmes such as the Quebec Skilled Worker Programme award high points to nurses.

The Filipino community has become well … **(Q11 integration)** into the fabric of Canadian society. In 2012, Tobias Enverga Jr became Canada's first senator of Filipino descent. Another Filipino-Canadian, Rey Pagtakhan, was … **(Q12 election)** to Parliament in 1998 and served as the Secretary of State for Asia and the Pacific from 2001 to 2004. Many members of Canada's Filipino community maintain strong ties with their home country, which in turn has led to a … **(Q13 strong)** of bilateral relations between Canada and the Philippines. As thousands of new temporary and permanent residents settle in Canada every year, this … **(Q14 connect)** will continue to strengthen and deepen.

(Canada Immigration Newsletter, January 2014; adapted and abridged)

0	*immigration* ✔

Q1 ....

Q2 ....

Q3 ....

Q4 ....

Q5 ....

Q6 ....

Q7 ....

Q8 ....

Q9 ....

Q10 ....

Q11 ....

Q12 ....

Q13 ....

Q14 ....

3 Migrating to the United States

a) Study the following text on immigration to the US and fill in the suitable words.

apply   contributions   enrich   legacy   loyalty   ~~parts~~   privileges   rewarded

The United States has a long history of welcoming immigrants from all ....parts........... **(1)** of the world. America values the .... **(2)** of immigrants who continue to .... **(3)** the country and preserve its .... **(4)** as a land of freedom and opportunity. People who have decided to become US citizens often refer to this decision as one of the most important ones in their lives. If they decide to .... **(5)** to become a US citizen, they will be showing their commitment to the United States and their .... **(6)** to its Constitution. In return, they are .... **(7)** with all the rights and .... **(8)** that are part of US citizenship.

b) Read the following text on the process of becoming a US citizen and find suitable words for the definitions printed below.

A guide to naturalisation

An individual may qualify for naturalisation if he or she is at least 18 years old, has been a permanent resident for at least five years and meets all other eligibility requirements.

5   Permanent residents are people who have "permanent resident" status in the United States and have received a so-called "Green Card". Yet it is not enough to be a permanent resident; they must also be in "continuous
10 residence" during that time. This means that they have not left the United States for a long period of time.

To be eligible for naturalisation they must be a person of good moral character with a
15 clean criminal record. Committing certain crimes may cause them to be ineligible for naturalisation.

If they do not tell the truth during their interview, the United States Citizenship and Immigration Services (USCIS) will deny their 20 application for lacking good moral character.

To be eligible for naturalisation, they must be able to read, write and speak basic English. They must also have a basic knowledge of US history and government (also known as 25 "civics"). Many schools and community organisations help people prepare for their naturalisation tests.

All applicants for naturalisation must be willing to support and defend the United 30 States and its Constitution. They declare their "attachment" to the United States and its Constitution when they take the Oath of Allegiance.

1. to be or become fit (as for an office); to meet the required standard: ...to qualify...............................

2. happening or existing without a break or interruption: ....

3. qualified or entitled to be chosen: ....

4. list of a person's previous criminal convictions: ....

5. to refuse to accept or admit sth.: ....

6. sb. who formally asks for sth. (such as admission to a college): ....

7. to say or state sth. in an official or public way: ....

8. formal and serious promise to tell the truth or to do sth.: ....

4 Language in use: Why immigrants are more successful than you

a) *You are going to read a text about the reasons for the economic success of immigrants. In most lines of the text there is a word that should not be there. Write that word in the space provided after each line. Some lines are correct. Indicate these lines with a tick (✓). There are two examples at the beginning.*

Do you love the four-hour workweek? Well, immigrants don't **do**! They don't — *do* — **0**
even believe in the forty-hour workweek. Instead of trying to figure out how — ✓ — **00**
they can work less hours each week, they try to figure out how they can work — **Q1**
in more hours. Sixty, seventy and even eighty hours are the numbers — **Q2**
immigrants also try to work each week. I know a few Indians who have two — **Q3**
full-time jobs, which means they are literally working with eighty hours — **Q4**
every week. And although working eighty hours a week doesn't give you the — **Q5**
best quality of life insurance, it gives you the potential to make more money. — **Q6**
By the way, it's easier to save money than to earn it. This is why immigrants — **Q7**
are frugal because when they understand that it is really hard to earn — **Q8**
money – especially if you are working eighty-hour weeks. They are never — **Q9**
afraid to ask other for discounts, because they know that if you never ask — **Q10**
you'll never receive calling. From negotiating at clothing stores to only — **Q11**
buying things that are on sale experts, immigrants always find ways to save — **Q12**
money. When times get tough the one thing that increases your odds of — **Q13**
success story is having a good education. Whether you are a teenage — **Q14**
immigrant or a middle-aged immigrant, it is never too late to go back to the — **Q15**
school. If you have a bachelor's degree, on average you'll make $900,000 — **Q16**
more over your lifetime than someone who just has seen a high school — **Q17**
diploma. And if you have a master's degree, you'll make $1,200,000 more in — **Q18**
your lifetime almost than a high school graduate. Apart from that, — **Q19**
immigrants never take neither "no" for an answer. Just because someone — **Q20**
tells you "no", it doesn't mean that you can't change that "no" to a "yes". — **Q21**
When my family first immigrated over here so my mum could not find — **Q22**
a job as a preschool teacher. So when they told her "no", why she told them — **Q23**
that she would work for free. Months later what they decided to hire her — **Q24**
and, more importantly, pay her. If someone tells you "no", it just means "not — **Q25**
right now". That "not right now" can turn you into a "yes" later on. — **Q26**

b) *Now read the conclusion of the text and underline all the different tense forms you detect. Can you explain why each tense form was used and what the author wants to express by using them?*

Have you heard the saying that the grass is greener on the other side? For immigrants, it usually is greener. Although they may not be living in a fancy home or a rich neighbour-
5 hood when they first immigrate, those living conditions are still better than the ones they came from. This is why they rarely complain about life because there really is nothing to be sad about. In their eyes, life is truly good. They
10 have a roof over their heads and their kids are getting a great education.

The next time you see an immigrant walking by, don't judge them because of their job, the way they talk or the clothes they wear. Be careful, as some of the richest immigrants 15 I know still drive their beat-up car that is fifteen years old and they buy their clothes from Wal-Mart, and only when they are on sale.

Immigrants are successful because of their 20 beliefs and the way they were brought up. So, take a page out of their book and learn a few things from them because it isn't too late for you to do so and, more importantly, to become successful. 25

(Neil Patel, *Quicksprout.com*, 30 June 2010; adapted and abridged)

One world

1 Word search

Split the text into words and phrases and match them with the definitions.

unprecedentedtransitiondeathtollthrive stepinstalemateresolveproblems~~reconciliation~~pursueproliferationproactiveperceptioninvigorateentaildisarmamentdevastatingdeployconcertedcapacityagenda

1. *reconciliation* : restoring friendly relations

2. ....: to prosper

3. ....: to become involved in a situation

4. ....: a situation in which progress is impossible

5. ....: to follow; to chase/seek to attain

6. ....: never done or known before

7. ....: ability, power

8. ....: number of casualties

9. ....: withdrawal of weapons

10. ....: highly damaging

11. ....: sudden increase in the amount of sth.

12. ....: controlling a situation rather than reacting to it

13. ....: to find a solution

14. ....: list of items to be discussed

15. ....: ability to see or hear

16. ....: to give strength/energy to

17. ....: jointly arranged/carried out

18. ....: to involve as a necessary consequence

19. ....: process of change

20. ....: to send troops to

2 Word families

a) *Fill the grid with verbs, nouns and adjectives where possible. Use a dictionary if necessary and translate the first word in each row.*

Verb	Noun (person)	Noun	Adjective	Meaning
to fail	failure	failure	failing	scheitern
to prevent	–			
to afford	–			
to maintain	–			
to promote			–	
–			humanitarian	
	–		ratified	
–	–		permanent	
	–		interdependent	
to endorse sth.	–			
to deter sb.	–			
to fluctuate	–			
–	–		adequate	
to annihilate	–			
	issuer	issue		
–		agency	–	
to perform				
	–	obligation		
	–	recommendation		

b) *Study the texts on pages 54 and 55 in* Prime Time 8 *and check how the words which have already been filled into the table are used in context.*

c) *Draw a table like the one above into your exercise book and find more words on these two pages that you can work with in the same way.*

3 Language in use: Médecins Sans Frontières wins Nobel Peace Prize

You are going to read a text about the French aid organisation Doctors Without Borders. Some words are missing from the text. Choose the correct answer (A, B, C or D) for each gap (1–12) in the text. Write your answers in the boxes provided. The first one (0) has been done for you.

In 1999 Médecins Sans Frontières, the French aid group, … **(0)** the Nobel Peace Prize for its pioneering work in disaster … **(Q1)** around the world. The secretive, five-member Nobel Committee said that giving the … **(Q2)** to the group, known in English as Doctors Without Borders, … **(Q3)** its "pioneering humanitarian work on several continents". It was the first Nobel Peace Prize given solely to an organisation since United Nations peacekeeping forces won in 1988.

"Médecins Sans Frontières has followed the fundamental principle that all disaster … **(Q4)** have a right to professional assistance, given as quickly and as … **(Q5)** as possible," committee chairman Francis Sejersted said in Oslo. Mr Sejersted praised the group as "fearless and self-sacrificing" and said they showed "each victim had a human face". … **(Q6)** in 1971, Médecins Sans Frontières calls itself the world's first non-military, non-governmental organisation to specialise in … **(Q7)** medical assistance.

MSF says it is active in 80 countries worldwide. By … **(Q8)** so rapidly in disasters, the Nobel committee said, Médecins Sans Frontières calls public attention to humanitarian catastrophes. "By pointing to the causes of such catastrophes, the organisation helps to form bodies of public opinion opposed to violations and abuses of power," the committee went on. "In … **(Q9)** situations, marked by violence and brutality, the humanitarian work of Médecins Sans Frontières enables the organisation to create openings for contacts between the … **(Q10)** parties. At the same time, each … **(Q11)** and self-sacrificing helper shows each victim a human face, stands for respect for that person's dignity, and is a source of hope for peace and … **(Q12)**," the committee said.

(Mark Tran, *The Guardian*, 15 October 1999; adapted and abridged)

0	A	has won	B	wins	C̸	won	D	was winning
Q1	A	relieve	B	relief	C	relay	D	relies
Q2	A	price	B	remuneration	C	reward	D	award
Q3	A	recognised	B	realised	C	relied	D	has realised
Q4	A	victories	B	victims	C	casualties	D	sacrifices
Q5	A	efficiently	B	effortlessly	C	affectionately	D	essentially
Q6	A	Found	B	Grounded	C	Ground	D	Founded
Q7	A	emergence	B	emergency	C	emerging	D	emerged
Q8	A	intervention	B	intervene	C	interventional	D	intervening
Q9	A	critic	B	criticised	C	critical	D	critique
Q10	A	opportunity	B	opportunistic	C	opposing	D	opportune
Q11	A	fearless	B	fearful	C	horrific	D	terrible
Q12	A	recommendation	B	reduction	C	reconstruction	D	reconciliation

0	Q1	Q2	Q3	Q4	Q5	Q6	Q7	Q8	Q9	Q10	Q11	Q12
C ✔												

4 Criticism of the role of the UN in international conflicts

Read through the text and find synonyms for the expressions below.

The charter of the creation of the United Nations was signed on 24 October 1945 to prevent further wars and to secure long-lasting peace around the world.

5 The UN Day, on which this anniversary is celebrated, brings to mind how the UN

10 began and the original vision of Franklin D. Roosevelt (FDR) and Winston Churchill.

15 The original intent was to create an international organisation that could promote and maintain peace throughout the world. The conception came to fruition after the most

20 disastrous global war in history, and being the second global war of the twentieth century, most of humanity welcomed the ideal of such an organisation in light of the failure of the previous League of Nations.

25 The concept of the United Nations was born from the ashes of World War II. FDR and Churchill believed the body was an absolute necessity if the world was to endure. The term

"United Nations" is first credited to FDR in referring to the allies who had joined together 30 to defeat Nazi Germany and its partners.

The core of the United Nations was actually the five major players: Great Britain, France, 35 Nationalist China, the Soviet Union and the United States. According to the charter of the UN, 40 these nations became the five permanent members of the Security Council, the organ at the heart of the 45 UN's effort to maintain stability and security in the world. The concept was sound, but like the League of Nations before it, the UN was founded with inherent, fundamental flaws.

The UN intended to pick up where the 50 League of Nations failed with world peace and the intent to create a more secure world. Yet without credibility or sufficient strength, a "world policeman" was bound to fail again.

(Dennis Jamison, *The Washington Times*, 25 October 2012; adapted and abridged)

1. to avert: *to prevent*...

2. to draw attention to: ....

3. the original plan: ....

4. most of mankind: ....

5. ruins: ....

6. organisation: ....

7. allies: ....

8. solid: ....

9. to continue: ....

10. had to fail: ....

5 Language in use: Oxfam – An international charity

You are going to read a text about Oxfam. In most lines of the text there is a word that should not be there. Write that word in the space provided after each line. Some lines are correct. Indicate these lines with a tick (✓). There are two examples at the beginning.

Oxfam, an international charity **ball** organisation, works on a number of	....ball....	0
vital issues to tackle the root causes of poverty, from life's basics – food,	✓	00
water, health organisation and education – to complex questions about	....	Q1
aid, climate change and human rights.	....	Q2
They're working towards a world where everyone else has enough to eat	....	Q3
and the opportunity to earn a decent living. With a water supply on tap,	....	Q4
food can grow up, and people can thrive.	....	Q5
Personal hygiene, affordable health care box and a quality education	....	Q6
are the foundations for a brighter future for poor people. In order	....	Q7
to achieve this noble objective it is vital to empower women to end	....	Q8
poverty. Consequently, women's rights are at the heart attack of their	....	Q9
work. However, it is clear to Oxfam that social engineering progress is	....	Q10
based on good business and means much more than making less	....	Q11
money. Companies can help lift up millions of people out of poverty if	....	Q12
they adhere to social principles.	....	Q13
Apart from these issues the Oxfam also has a long record of saving	....	Q14
lives in a crisis. When conflicts or natural disasters strike, they step	....	Q15
in to help. Good, effective aid workers saves lives and helps poor people	....	Q16
work their own way out of poverty trap.	....	Q17
One in five people in Britain lives in poverty. That's about 13 million	....	Q18
people. So they have this problem on their agenda and are	....	Q19
not working to support them.	....	Q20
In more addition, Oxfam helps vulnerable people fight discrimination	....	Q21
and demands their rights.	....	Q22
Even environmental problems (e.g. reducing the impact of global	....	Q23
outside warming) are being dealt with by Oxfam.	....	Q24

6 Synonyms

Match the words on the left with the correct definitions or examples on the right.

1.	prosperity	D	A splits
2.	divisions		B to maintain in its original state
3.	diversity		C lasting, enduring
4.	to uphold		D̸ wealth
5.	to preserve		E to produce sth. mechanically and in large quantities
6.	sustainable		F to defend
7.	to churn out		G variety

The individual and society

1 Maslow's hierarchy of needs

According to humanistic psychologist Abraham Maslow, our actions are motivated by the desire to fulfil certain needs. His theory suggests that the fulfilment of basic needs has priority over meeting other, more advanced needs.

This hierarchy is most often displayed as a pyramid. The lowest levels of the pyramid are made up of the most basic needs, while the more complex needs are located at the top of the pyramid.

a) Fill in suitable words from the box into the pyramid below (see Prime Time 8, *page 66 if you need help).*

acceptance • accomplishment • affection • ~~air~~ • belonging • companionship • esteem • ~~food~~ • fulfilling one's potential • healthcare • love • personal growth • personal worth • ~~physiological~~ • safe neighbourhood • safety • security • self-actualising • shelter from the environment • sleep • social recognition • steady employment • water

5. .... needs:

4. .... needs:

3. .... needs:

2. .... needs:

1. ....Physiological........ needs: *air, food*

b) The words and phrases below are synonyms of elements from the text about Maslow's theory (1–4) and the pyramid above (5–10). Fill in the correct words.

Word	Synonym	Word	Synonym
1. ranking	*hierarchy*	**6.** kindness	
2. driven		**7.** capacity	
3. fundamental		**8.** cover	
4. elaborate		**9.** acknowledgement	
5. achievement		**10.** stable	

2 Volunteering

a) There are some strange jobs you can do if you want to be a volunteer in Britain. Write short job descriptions using the words in brackets.

Volunteer job	Description	
1. beach watcher	*organise the cleaning of the beaches*	(cleaning)
2. kids theatre volunteer		(plays)
3. neighbour dispute mediator		(local clashes)
4. resuscitation trainer		(life support skills)
5. tandem bike rider		(blind people)
6. toad warden		(breeding season)

b) Look at the words below. Which ones have something to do with volunteering according to your view?

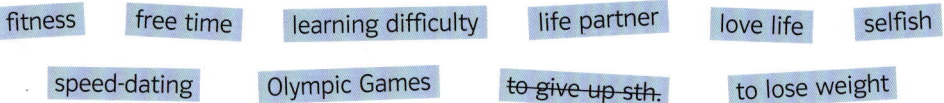

fitness   free time   learning difficulty   life partner   love life   selfish

speed-dating   Olympic Games   ~~to give up sth.~~   to lose weight

c) Fill in suitable words from above into the text on volunteering below.

Doing some form of voluntary work has never been more popular with British people. Over 20 million people were engaged in voluntary activities in 2013.

Volunteering means ....*giving up*............ **(1)** time to do work of benefit to the community. It can take many forms, from helping children with

.... **(2)**, working in an animal hospital or planting trees. London, which hosted the 2012 .... **(3)**, needed more than 70,000 volunteers to help ensure the games were a success.

Volunteers can be anyone of any age. Students and full-time workers alike often manage to squeeze in some volunteer work. But what motivates volunteers? Some do it out of a sense of altruism while others find they have .... **(4)** available. But in this .... **(5)** age more are asking what they can get out of it. Some mention self-awareness. Others mention the opportunity to get to know people they would not normally meet.

A relatively new phenomenon is the hope of meeting new friends or even a .... **(6)** through volunteering. In a recent survey 20% of 18- to 24-year-olds and 8% of over-65s said their .... **(7)** had improved since they began volunteering. "Volunteering is what .... **(8)** promises but never fulfils – a way of seeing a lot of truth about someone you've just met in as short a time as possible," one of the volunteers interviewed mentioned. The same poll found that nearly half of volunteers enjoyed improved health and .... **(9)**, a quarter had .... **(10)** – especially those working with children or doing conservation projects – and two thirds felt less stressed. So, it seems volunteering may improve your life – you may even find the person of your dreams.

3 Language in use: Personal freedom

You are going to read a text about current living patterns among women. Some words are missing from the text. Choose from the list (A–L) the correct part for each gap (1–9) in the text. There are two extra words you should not use. Write your answers in the boxes provided. The first one (0) has been done for you.

Georgie Roles is only 32 and she has decided "to be … **(0)** for ever". It's not that she hasn't had boyfriends. She lived with two of them in … **(Q1)** that lasted about five years each, and her most recent boyfriend was around for 18 months. No, she says, it's to do with the realisation that her experience of life is … **(Q2)** and more fulfilling when she is free to live alone and as she chooses. Roles works as an airline pilot. She qualified in 1999 and now flies Boeing 737s, 757s and 767s for a leading British airline. If this wasn't achievement enough, she spends her weekends as a skydiving coach and was in a team that almost made it to the World Championships in Formation Skydiving in 2012.

Roles grew up thinking that men would … **(Q3)** her for doing what she was good at: "The more successful you are, the more attractive you are." Her experience proved otherwise. "I got the impression with a couple of them that the idea of going out with me was great, because they could say to their mates, 'I'm going out with a skydiving pilot.' But the reality was that they couldn't cope with it." Her first boyfriend gave her an … **(Q4)**: flying or him. "I said to him, 'I think your bags are on top of the wardrobe.' The choice was obvious, but the consequences made me sad – that I lose someone to carry on being myself."

There has been a dramatic increase in the number of single women, according to the Office for National Statistics. The number of 18- to 49-year-olds living alone has more than doubled over the past three decades. Dubbed "freemales" and "quirkyalones", these women tend to be successful metropolitans – the … **(Q5)** of sad, single women waiting for Mr Right. Jan MacVarish, a sociologist from the University of Kent, who has spent several years researching the lives of single women aged 30 to 50, believes that the paradigm has shifted. "Women in modern Britain no longer need the … **(Q6)** of marriage or a partnership to feed themselves, get a house or have sex. They earn their own money; buy their own homes. … **(Q7)** to a mortgage has become more of an adult marker than commitment to a husband or child," she says.

The idea that relationships are … **(Q8)** to self-development is very common. "There is a sense that you have to love yourself before anyone can love you – that sounds like a trite self-helpism, but it's a really common idea – that you can't function in a relationship without being a fully functioning emotional individual yourself, and that it is something you work on by yourself – that is a huge shift," she explains. "It's not just that … **(Q9)** provides an opportunity for self-exploration, but that self-exploration should take priority within or over relationships."

(Sally Williams, *The Telegraph*, 19 September 2010; adapted and abridged)

A	admire	**F**	institution	**K**	singleness	**0**	✓	**Q5**
B	antithesis	**G**	obvious	**L**	ultimatum	**Q1**		**Q6**
C	commitment	**H**	relationships			**Q2**		**Q7**
D	emotional	**I**	richer			**Q3**		**Q8**
E	hostile	**J**	single			**Q4**		**Q9**

4 The American Dream

The concept of the American Dream probably has a different meaning to every US citizen. For some it is the dream of freedom and equality, for others it is the dream of a fulfilled life or even of fame and wealth. In general, the American dream can be defined as being the opportunity for and the freedom of all citizens to achieve their goals and become rich and successful if only they work hard enough. It focuses more on the success of the individual and not primarily on the well-being of the whole population.

a) Below are a number of words that can be associated with the American Dream. Group them into three categories. Before you sort the words you will have to think about what your categories will be.

> baby-boomer • to be blessed with sth. • civil rights • country of boundless possibilities • distance • equality of opportunity • fortune • freedom • gender equality • glory • heritage • liberty • minority group • nation • to pass a law • patriotism • persistent • poverty • powerful • proud • to pursue a dream • rags-to-riches • road to success • to roll up your sleeves • social climbing • Stars and Stripes • success • tolerance • wealth

Category 1:	Category 2:	Category 3: ....

b) Choose one category and draw a mind map which shows the connections between the words. Go online and add more suitable words.

c) Complete the following quotes on the American Dream with suitable words from above.

1. "I think the American Dream says that anything can happen if you work hard enough at it, are ....**persistent**........ and have some ability. The sky is the limit to what you can build and what can happen to you and your family." *(Sanford I. Weill)*

2. "If .... Americans can be who they are and boldly stand at the altar with who they love then surely, surely we can give everyone in this country a fair chance at that great American Dream." *(Michelle Obama)*

3. "I am living proof that the American dream still exists. It is still alive and well. There is only one trick, you have to be willing to .... and work very, very hard." *(Paula Deen)*

4. "I have spent my life judging the .... between American reality and the American dream." *(Bruce Springsteen)*

5. "The .... is not easy to navigate, but with hard work, drive and passion, it's possible to achieve the American dream." *(Tommy Hilfiger)*

6. "The negative side of the American Dream comes when people pursue .... at any cost, which in turn destroys the vision and the dream." *(Azar Nafisi)*

5 Expressing yourself in the right register

a) The text below uses both formal and informal expressions. Complete the table with suitable counterparts taken from the text and think about the effect the use of the different registers may have on the reader.

Passers-by mainly blow me off, a homeless woman sitting on the sidewalk or a bench. The people who do pick my brains are either curious, or they give me useless advice. Many
5 people also assume that the homeless are all drug addicts, criminals or prostitutes and disregard me on purpose. I am none of these things, yet I have seen the stereotypes
10 first-hand.

I don't have recent data, but I know that in 1994, a study of homeless people in Manhattan was published
15 and a summary appeared in many newspapers. The findings said that 30–40% of the street homeless population suffered from a mental illness,
20 including alcoholism and drug addiction. It's a tragic statistic, but you can also infer from this survey that 60–70% of the street homeless are not mentally ill, drug addicts or alcoholics. People should remember that other factors –
25 such as education, job training, employment, the housing market and how programmes for the poor are administered – also cause people to end up on the streets.

I am often asked if I have enough to eat. I
30 will chow down anything that is healthful. People who work with food bring leftovers to me. Soup kitchens are also an alternative. The volunteers work to make it pleasant and serve edible food. I take nourishment thankfully.
35 There are many people with poor table

manners, unhygienic habits or looking for a fight. There are hardly any goombahs, sadly. If you want the truth, shelters, soup kitchens and other facilities for the poor are the most unsanitary, unhealthy and dangerous places I 40 have ever been to.

I have seen some of the best and worst of humanity since I became homeless a few years before the 45 recession. My belongings have been cabbaged by other residents and workers at the shelters and even church personnel and 50 pedestrians. One time, my purse, which I kept inside a backpack, was taken without permission. It contained a lot of information about confidants and relatives 55 and other personal papers. You cannot replace those.

I don't want to sound like I am whining. I have also met people like a young woman who saw me upset after an attack by a resident 60 of the Park Avenue women's shelter. She required to know if she could help me. I told her how I had lost my apartment, what the shelters were like, and previous work I had done. She was focused, patient, a good 65 listener and gave me cash. The young woman's unselfish behaviour, compassionate heart and generous spirit allowed me to walk away fresh. She was exceptional.

(Mary, *The Guardian*, 13 October 2013; adapted and abridged)

Informal register		Formal register
1. to blow sb. off	to ignore sb.	
2.	to ask sb. sth.	
3.	to eat	
4.	a friend	
5.	to steal sth.	

b) Which other words and expressions seem formal or informal to you?

Big money

1 Proverbs and sayings

Match the two columns.

#	Left	Box	Letter	Right
1.	A fool and his money are soon parted.	G	A	Don't risk losing everything by putting all your efforts or all your money into one plan.
2.	A penny saved is a penny earned.		B	Even the richest people cannot take their money with them after death.
3.	Cut your coat according to your cloth.		C	Not paying back the money you have borrowed will not reduce what you owe other people.
4.	Don't put all your eggs in one basket.		D	Money is not earned easily. In most cases you have to work for it.
5.	Forgetting a debt does not pay it.		E	It is useful to save money that you already have since it is hard to earn more.
6.	He who pays the piper calls the tune.		F	Plan your activities in line with your resources so that you can get by with what you have.
7.	Money doesn't grow on trees.		G	Stupid people spend money without thinking about it enough and so they will lose it quickly.
8.	You can't take it with you when you go.		H	The person who provides the money can decide how it should be spent.

2 Language in use: Compulsive shopping

You are going to read a text about shopaholics. In most lines of the text there is a word that should not be there. Write that word in the space provided after each line. Some lines are correct. Indicate these lines with a tick (✓). There are two examples at the beginning.

For most of us **the** shopping is more than just going out and getting	*the*	0
something we need. Shopping has become an event, a pastime,	✓	00
a hobby which we look forward to us even if we don't buy anything		Q1
on one of our shopping mall sprees.		Q2
Compulsive shopping, however, is much more than that. Shopaholics		Q3
go out and buy good things to relieve some form of anxiety. So shopping		Q4
becomes an addiction and later on this idea often leads to attempts to		Q5
cover it up. But what are the only causes of this behaviour? Explanations		Q6
range from emotional deprivation in childhood fantasy to the need to		Q7
gain control room, from the inability to tolerate negative feelings to		Q8
perfectionism. In many cases the compulsive shoppers want to impress,		Q9
to seek approval or excitement. So the act of buying something is often		Q10
not an aim in itself, it is a means to achieve recognition and respect.		Q11
So if you are not susceptible to compulsive shopping, follow a few simple		Q12
rules: Make a shopping list before going out to prevent yourself from		Q13
buying things you don't need. Avoid yourself big shopping centres or		Q14
malls because you might feel tempted to spend out. Think twice before		Q15
you buy something and ask if you really need it.		Q16

3 Word families

a) Study the table below and underline the words that you would not have thought of. Look up the words you do not fully understand.

able	ability, disability, enable, disable, disabled, …
to continue	continuous, continuously, continuity, discontinue, …
to decide	decision, decisive, decisively, undecided, …
to depend	dependent, independent, dependency, independency, …
to differ	different, differently, difference, indifferent, indifferently, indifference, differentiate, differentiation, …
equal	equality, inequality, unequal, unequally, equally, equalise, equaliser, …
happy	happily, unhappy, unhappily, happiness, unhappiness, …
to reside	resident, residence, residency, residual, residue, …
sign	signify, significance, insignificance, significant, insignificant, …
social	society, sociology, socialite, socialist, socialism, anti-social, …

b) Write a similar table for the words below. You can also use a mind map like the one below to collect ideas.

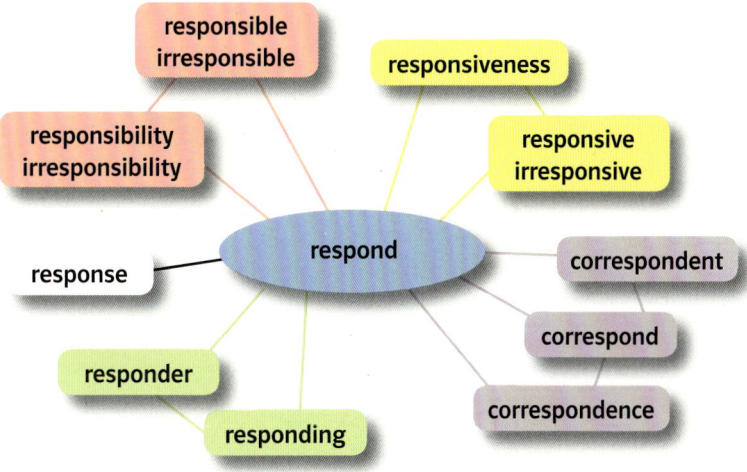

to respond	
to add	
to defend	
to judge	

4 Language in use: Daniel Kahneman on income

You are going to read a text about the inequality of income. Some words are missing from the text. Use the words in brackets to complete each gap (1–15) in the text. Write your answers in the spaces provided at the end of the text. The first one (0) has been done for you.

… (**0 educate**) is an important factor of income – one of the most important – but it is less important than most people think. If everyone had the same education, the … (**Q1 equal**) of income would be reduced by less than 10%. When you focus on education you neglect all the other factors that … (**Q2 determination**) income. The differences of income among people who have the same education are huge.

Income is an important factor of people's … (**Q3 satisfy**) with their lives, but it is far less important than most people think. If everyone had the same income, the … (**Q4 differ**) among people in life satisfaction would be reduced by less than 5%.

Income is even less important as a determinant of emotional … (**Q5 happy**). Winning the lottery is a happy event, but the excitement does not last. On average, individuals with high income are in a better mood than people with lower income, but the difference is about one third as large as most people expect. When you think of rich and poor people, your thoughts are … (**Q6 evitable**) focused on circumstances in which their income is important. But happiness depends on other factors more than it depends on income.

People who are paralysed due to spinal injury are often … (**Q7 happy**), but they are not unhappy all the time because they spend most of the time … (**Q8 experience**) and thinking about other things than their … (**Q9 able**). When we think of what it is like to be paralysed, or blind, or a lottery winner or a … (**Q10 reside**) of California we focus on the … (**Q11 distinguish**) aspects of each of these conditions. The mismatch of focusing on thinking about a life condition and actually living it is the cause of the "focusing illusion".

Marketers exploit the focusing illusion. When people are led to believe that they "must have" a good, they … (**Q12 great**) exaggerate the difference that the good will make to the quality of their life. The focusing illusion is greater for some goods than for others, … (**Q13 depend**) on the extent to which the goods attract … (**Q14 continue**) attention over time. The focusing illusion is, for example, likely to be more … (**Q15 signify**) for leather car seats than for books on tape.

(Daniel Kahneman, *edge.org*, 2014; adapted and abridged)

0	*education* ✔	Q8	....
Q1	....	Q9	....
Q2	....	Q10	....
Q3	....	Q11	....
Q4	....	Q12	....
Q5	....	Q13	....
Q6	....	Q14	....
Q7	....	Q15	....

5 Language in use: Using social media for marketing

You are going to read a text about the use of social media in marketing. Some words are missing from the text. Choose the correct answer (A, B, C or D) for each gap (1–12) in the text. Write your answers in the boxes provided. The first one (0) has been done for you.

Using social … **(0)** for marketing can enable small businesses to further their reach to more customers. Your customers are … **(Q1)** with brands through social media, therefore, having a strong social media presence on the web is the … **(Q2)** to tap into their interest. If implemented correctly, marketing with social media can bring … **(Q3)** success to your business.

Social media marketing is a form of internet marketing that implements various social media networks in order to achieve marketing communication and branding goals. Social media marketing primarily covers … **(Q4)** involving social sharing of content, videos and images for marketing purposes.

Before you begin creating social media marketing … **(Q5)**, consider your business' goals. Starting a social media marketing campaign without a plan in mind is like … **(Q6)** through a forest without a map – you'll only end up lost. Create a social media marketing plan and brainstorm about your … **(Q7)**: What are you hoping to achieve through social media marketing? Who is your … **(Q8)** audience? Where would your target … **(Q9)** hang out and how would they use social media? What message do you want to send to your audience with social media marketing?

… **(Q10)** with other areas of online marketing, content is king when it comes to social media marketing. Make sure you are offering … **(Q11)** information that your ideal customers will find interesting. Create a variety of content by implementing images, videos and infographics in … **(Q12)** to classic text-based content.

(Larry Kim, *wordstream.com*; adapted and abridged)

0	**A**	medial	**B**	median	**C̸**	media	**D**	medic
Q1	**A**	recognising	**B**	interacting	**C**	reacting	**D**	realising
Q2	**A**	closet	**B**	solution	**C**	key	**D**	keynote
Q3	**A**	marking	**B**	remarkable	**C**	remarking	**D**	remaking
Q4	**A**	activities	**B**	activism	**C**	auctioning	**D**	attention
Q5	**A**	campers	**B**	camps	**C**	strategists	**D**	campaigns
Q6	**A**	wandering	**B**	wondering	**C**	wonder	**D**	wander
Q7	**A**	tales	**B**	goals	**C**	gaols	**D**	tolls
Q8	**A**	end	**B**	target	**C**	tail	**D**	entail
Q9	**A**	public	**B**	publication	**C**	publican	**D**	audience
Q10	**A**	Consistent	**B**	Inconsistent	**C**	Controlling	**D**	Checking
Q11	**A**	worth	**B**	worthy	**C**	valuably	**D**	valuable
Q12	**A**	action	**B**	addition	**C**	excess	**D**	agenda

0	Q1	Q2	Q3	Q4	Q5	Q6	Q7	Q8	Q9	Q10	Q11	Q12
C✓												

6 Language in use: Consumerism among children

a) You are going to read a text about children as consumers. Some words are missing from the text. Choose from the list (A–P) the correct part for each gap (1–13) in the text. There are two extra words you should not use. Write your answers in the boxes provided. The first one (0) has been done for you.

There is no doubt that children have enormous … **(0)** power, both directly and indirectly. On the one hand many of them have large … **(Q1)** of money to spend, on the other hand they are able to persuade and … **(Q2)** parents on what to buy.

This may be due to the fact that parents often give in to their children's … **(Q3)** because they do not have the … **(Q4)** to say no. After all, if the money is around there does not seem to be a major problem. However, if the family is short of money, the situation is awkward for parents and children alike. Children want to keep up with their … **(Q5)** and parents do not want to reject their children's wishes. But what can you do if you simply cannot … **(Q6)** what you would like to buy?

… **(Q7)** and marketing experts know about the power of children and … **(Q8)** this aspect as best they can. Children are being … **(Q9)** specifically – either to influence their parents or to become loyal customers once they have grown up.

When it became apparent that children under the age of ten are unable to distinguish between commercials and regular TV programmes, states like Sweden … **(Q10)** advertising during children's prime time. It is extremely … **(Q11)** that even one single exposure to a TV advert might change the consumer habits of a child for a long time, if not forever, as brand names and slogans are firmly … **(Q12)** on a child's memory.

Such long-term strategies are the … **(Q13)** of advertising, making sure that future consumers choose the right product from the right company.

A	advertisers	**H**	exploit	**O**	targeted	**0**	✓	**Q7**	
B	afford	**I**	imprinted	**P**	worrying	**Q1**		**Q8**	
C	amounts	**J**	influence			**Q2**		**Q9**	
D	backbone	**K**	negotiation			**Q3**		**Q10**	
E	banned	**L**	nerve			**Q4**		**Q11**	
F	busy	**M**	peers			**Q5**		**Q12**	
G	demands	**N**	purchasing			**Q6**		**Q13**	

b) Find synonyms for these expressions in the text above.

1. undoubtedly: …*there is no doubt*……………………………………………

2. to win approval or support for: ……………………………………………

3. side: ………………………………………………………………………………

4. TV commercial: …………………………………………………………………

5. person who buys sth.: …………………………………………………………

6. specific name of a company: …………………………………………………

7. plans of action: …………………………………………………………………

Science and technology

1 Surveillance and the media

a) *Take one element from each column and form sentences on surveillance and the media. Add your own ideas if you like.*

Column 1	Column 2	Column 3
~~to analyse~~ to carry out to collect to gather to intercept to process to spark to tighten to unscramble	~~data on~~ a debate on a domestic surveillance programme on (encrypted) messages on a full-body scan on information on security on	airline passengers electronic communication federal power internet activities phone calls privacy social networking websites ~~suspicious activities~~ the surveillance of citizens unreasonable searches

1. Their job was to analyse data on suspicious activities on government servers.
2.
3.
4.
5.
6.

b) *Fill in suitable words into the text below. Make sure you use the correct form.*

to accuse sb. of sth.   address   to articulate sth.   boundary   detail   invasion
~~to obtain sth.~~   to promote sth.   to publish sth.   record   subscriber   uncomfortable

You are the editor of a local newspaper. A reporter on your staff comes to you having
...........obtained........... (1) (by legal means) one of the following:

- police .... (2) of arrests for drunken driving
- the personal .... (3) of the employees of local clinics which perform abortions
- the .... (4) list of a survivalist magazine with pronounced racist overtones
- the donors to a group that .... (5) gay rights
- the names of husbands .... (6) of infidelity in divorce suits, along with the identities of their alleged lovers
- .... (7) of homes where pit bulls are kept

The reporter proposes to .... (8) the names and home addresses and map them on a large graphic, all part of an article on "The drunks/abortionists/racists/gays/cheats/scary dogs next door". Some of these lists might strike you as fair game. Others probably make you
.... (9) or indignant. You might find that the tricky part is .... (10) why: what are the .... (11) between a public service and an .... (12) of privacy?

c) *Write a short paragraph that answers the question at the end of the text.*

● **2** **Language in use: How big brother spies on pupils**

You are going to read a text about school surveillance. Some words are missing from the text. Choose the correct answer (A, B, C or D) for each gap (1–10) in the text. Write your answers in the boxes provided. The first one (0) has been done for you.

Lockdown High, a new book by Annette Fuentes, cites cases of school … **(0)** that are mind-boggling: A student from Arizona strip-searched because Ibuprofen, a widely used painkiller, was not allowed under her school rules; the school in Texas where teachers can carry … **(Q1)** handguns; and the Philadelphia school that gave its pupils laptops equipped with a secret feature allowing them to be … **(Q2)** on outside classroom hours.

Just about all the schools Fuentes writes about are united by a belief in the principle of "… **(Q3)** tolerance". And, as she sees it, their neurotic emphasis on security has plenty of negative results: It renders the atmosphere in schools tense and fragile, and threatens to define young people's life chances at an early age – because, as she puts it, "suspensions and academic failure are strong predictors of entry into the criminal justice system". There is also, of course, the small matter of personal … **(Q4)**.

It would be comforting to think of all this as a peculiarly American phenomenon. But in the UK, we seem almost as keen on turning schools into authoritarian fortresses. One in seven schools has insisted on students being fingerprinted. Security systems based on face … **(Q5)** have already been piloted in ten schools, and on-site police officers are now a common feature of the education system. Most omnipresent of all are … **(Q6)** cameras: 85% of secondary schools are reckoned to use them, even in changing rooms and toilets.

Now, as the surveillance state embeds itself in the lives of millions of children, the education bill currently making its way through parliament promises to extend teachers' powers to search pupils. Teachers will be able not just to … **(Q7)** phones and computers, but … **(Q8)** them of any data if they think there "is a good reason to do so", thereby giving them new powers to … **(Q9)** pupils and issue summary expulsions. Education secretary Michael Gove casts all this as a matter of common sense. "Our bill will put heads and teachers back in control, giving them a range of tough new powers to deal with bullies and the most … **(Q10)** pupils," he said last year, before he used a very telling phrase: "Heads will be able to take a zero-tolerance approach."

(John Harris, *The Guardian*, 9 June 2011; adapted and abridged)

0	A	surveillance	B	examination	C	spying	D	negligence
Q1	A	unwrapped	B	concealed	C	masked	D	sheltered
Q2	A	spied	B	spotted	C	observed	D	overheard
Q3	A	nil	B	nought	C	zero	D	blank
Q4	A	sanctuary	B	privacy	C	disguise	D	isolation
Q5	A	sensibility	B	acceptance	C	admission	D	recognition
Q6	A	guard	B	safeguard	C	safeness	D	security
Q7	A	seize	B	embrace	C	lay hands	D	release
Q8	A	wipe	B	remove	C	clean off	D	clarify
Q9	A	abandon	B	forsake	C	restrain	D	prevent
Q10	A	courteous	B	painful	C	disruptive	D	combative

0	Q1	Q2	Q3	Q4	Q5	Q6	Q7	Q8	Q9	Q10
A✔										

3 Genetic engineering

a) Choose the correct word in each pair and write down the sentence.

British scientists at the University of Sheffield Centre for Stem Cell Biology have (***announced • denounced***) **(1)** that it may one day be possible to clone human eggs and (***spam • sperm***) **(2)** from stem cells. This means the entire process of human (***conception • perception***) **(3)** could take place in a science laboratory. It would revolutionise fertility treatments for (***couples • couplets***) **(4)** unable to have children of their own as well as enable same-sex couples to have children that (***shape · share***) **(5)** the genetic code of both partners.

Fertility scientists (***described • inscribed***) **(6)** the research as an exciting step forward. The (***earliest • latest***) **(7)** findings are believed to have huge implications for the way studies that investigate the (***processes • production***) **(8)** of egg and sperm development can be (***overtaken • undertaken***) **(9)**. Nevertheless, we are still in the early stages of fully understanding the biology of conception. Up to now, scientists cannot entirely explain why some men and women are (***impotent • infertile***) **(10)**, which means that they cannot produce sperm and eggs of their own.

b) You are going to read a text about human cloning. In most lines of the text there is a word that should not be there. Write that word in the space provided after each line. Some lines are correct. Indicate these lines with a tick (✓). There are two examples at the beginning.

On 5 July 1996, the most famous **of** sheep in modern history was born.	*of*	**0**
Ian Wilmut and a group of Scottish scientists announced that they had	✓	**00**
been successfully cloned a sheep named Dolly. If you stood Dolly beside	....	**Q1**
a "naturally" conceived sheep, you wouldn't notice any differences	....	**Q2**
between the two. While Dolly's birth certificate marked an incredible	....	**Q3**
scientific breakthrough, it also set off questions in the scientific and global	....	**Q4**
community about what – or who – might be next time to be "duplicated."	....	**Q5**
Cloning sheep and other nonhuman beings seemed more ethically	....	**Q6**
benign to some than potentially cloning people. Re-engineering the	....	**Q7**
human inside reproductive process has made many people nervous that	....	**Q8**
although cloning crosses the ethical boundaries of science. But we can't	....	**Q9**
fully evaluate across the moral dilemma without first addressing the	....	**Q10**
potential benefits of human cloning before. Therapeutic cloning holds the	....	**Q11**
most promise of valuable medical advancement. Therapeutic cloning is	....	**Q12**
the process by which a person's DNA is not used to grow an embryonic	....	**Q13**
clone. However, instead of inserting this embryo also into a surrogate	....	**Q14**
mother, its cells are used to grow out stem cells. These stem cells could	....	**Q15**
become the basis for customised human repair kits. They can grow	....	**Q16**
replacement organs, such as hearts, livers and her skin. And since the	....	**Q17**
stem cells would come from embryo clones using your own cell's DNA,	....	**Q18**
your body would not readily accept them. Yet, some scientists believe	....	**Q19**
a today's technology just isn't ready to be tested on humans. Cloning	....	**Q20**
technology is nevertheless still in its early stages, and nearly 98 per cent of	....	**Q21**
cloning efforts moreover end in failure. Opponents of cloning point out	....	**Q22**
that while we can euthanise defective clones of other animals shelters, it's	....	**Q23**
morally problematic if this happens during the human cloning process.	....	**Q24**

4 Foods with benefits

a) *Read the article below and underline all of the words and phrases that describe the quality and the benefits of various food items.*

Start in Aisle 2: Here is grape juice for your heart. In Aisle 5: Vitamin-packed water for your immune system. In aisle after aisle, wonders beckon. Foods and drinks to help
5 your heart, lower your cholesterol, trim your tummy. Toss them into your cart and you might feel better. You might even live longer.

Or not. Because this, shoppers, is the question: Are all
10 these products really healthy, or are some of them just hyped? Over the past decade, functional food has turned into a big business. And more Americans
15 are buying into the functional story. But as sales soar, federal regulators worry that some packaged foods that scream healthy on their labels are in fact no healthier than many ordinary brands. They have been cracking
20 down on products that, in their view, make dubious claims and bamboozle shoppers with slick marketing.

No one is saying that these products are unsafe or unhealthy, or that there isn't science
25 behind them. But nutritionists say that the vast number of functional foods has left many consumers confused about the products' actual health value. And, in some cases, manufacturers are bending or even breaking
30 the rules about how they market these

products. Companies promote myriad processed foods that have been loaded with vitamins and nutrients, or contain a potentially beneficial ingredient, as wellness aids. For many, these "healthified" foods have 35 become the new health food. Many Americans are willing to pay a premium for ready-to-heat and on-the-go foods that seem to promise shortcuts to healthier living. 40

However, the bureau of consumer protection is concerned that people who buy foods that, for instance, claim to bolster immunity or reduce the risk of 45 prostate cancer might forgo a flu shot or a doctor's visit.

The situation is clearer in Europe, where authorities have set up an independent panel of experts to check every health claim. Food 50 makers submit applications with scientific evidence for a specific claim. The panel then reviews each case and issues an opinion on whether the evidence shows that eating the food indeed causes the advertised effect. A list 55 of approved health claims is intended to make food shopping less confusing – at least for consumers in Europe.

(Natasha Singer, *The New York Times*, 14 May 2011; adapted and abridged)

b) *Sort your findings into three categories: Words and phrases that carry a positive meaning and are used to advertise the respective food items, those that describe the food items in a comparatively neutral way, and words and phrases that carry a negative meaning.*

c) *Go back to the article and find phrases that mean the same as the words below.*

Word	Synonym
1. full of vitamins	*vitamin-packed*
2. to lure and attract attention	
3. to change into sth.	
4. to accept sth. as valid	
5. to put limits on sb. or sth.	

Word	Synonym
6. to deceive sb. by trickery or flattery	
7. of an indefinitely great number	
8. supposedly healthy	
9. only requires heating up	
10. to do without sth.	

5 The language of science: Location-based apps and the future of shopping

a) *Read the following text and highlight the features that are common in scientific texts.*

b) *Find out which tenses are most frequent.*

It is a current trend that more and more smartphone apps require access to location data provided by the phone's built-in GPS module. According to a 2012 report, three-
5 quarters of America's smartphone owners use their devices to retrieve information related to their location. Such location data is promising to advertisers. They can begin sending customers so-called hyperlocal advertising,
10 tailored not just to the city, but to a particular city block.

The technology is called "geofencing", which has been used for years in the ankle
15 bracelets worn by accused criminals under constant surveillance. A judge might grant a criminal suspect permission to go to her job, her church and her
20 local supermarket, with each approved location plugged into the court's computer system. Data from the ankle-strapped GPS could confirm that the suspect was staying out of mischief or send a warning to police when
25 she went to a prohibited location.

Geofencing also has other uses, for example for parents who want to know about their children's whereabouts. The service retrieves location data from a child's phone
30 and sends a message whenever the child arrives at home or at school or leaves again.

When marketers build a geofence, they have no desire to restrict customers'

movements. The goal is to detect people's close approach to a nearby business that is 35 looking to make a sale, so the company can ping customers with a text message urging them to buy. Because marketers realise that nobody wants a constant stream of text messages, a policy of "frequency capping" is 40 practiced. Customers generally get no more than five messages a week, even if many other attractive deals come within range.

Still, geofencing is rarely 45 used by advertisers nowadays. The technology requires constantly recalculating the phone's position, which shortens 50 battery life quickly. Yet, even if geofencing becomes more energy efficient, it might still not be a sound strategy for selling many consumer products.

As psychologists found out, valuable 55 things are usually not consumed spontaneously. It is highly unlikely that a customer, alerted by his phone that a half-price sale on expensive consumer technology is taking place in a store nearby, will act upon 60 sudden impulse and seriously consider the offer. Even at the lower price, such items will cost hundreds of dollars and are thus the sort of purchase consumers think about and plan for. 65

(Hiawatha Bray, *discover.com*, 30 April 2014; adapted and abridged)

c) *Complete the sentences below with suitable words from the article.*

1. Facebook plans to use ....Location data......... from its mobile apps to customise the ads it serves consumers.

2. It can record video, access e-mail and .... from the web by connecting wirelessly to a user's mobile phone.

3. You can use your smartphone to track your car's location, get information on its condition and use .... to manage mileage.

4. We live in an age of .... where our words and actions can be made public by anyone with a mobile phone and an internet connection.

5. This short guide gives some examples of successful communication activities to help the project participants to develop a .... for communicating about their work.

6. Hamlet is the exact opposite; he is very hesitant, and does not act ....

Ideals and reality

1 Synonyms

Match the two columns.

1. to admit	G	**A**	public expression of protest	
2. burden		**B**	to enter a party without an invitation	
3. candidly		**C**	to have the impression	
4. compulsory		**D**	courtship	
5. controversial		**E**	self-imposed control over books and their content	
6. to deflect		**F**	breach of law	
7. to flatter		**G**	to confess	
8. frank		**H**	giving rise to disagreement	
9. to gatecrash		**I**	very great in amount	
10. mating ritual		**J**	openly	
11. offence		**K**	very angry	
12. outraged		**L**	part of your duty	
13. overwhelming		**M**	to cause to change direction	
14. self-censorship		**N**	open, honest	
15. to suspect		**O**	heavy load	
16. uproar		**P**	to say nice things about sb.	

2 Finding opposites

Find opposites and write them down in the table below. Some adjectives have more than one opposite.

~~active~~	aggressive	biased	defensive	sincere
formal	funny	humorous	informal	ironic
matter-of-fact	~~passive~~	sarcastic	serious	fair

Adjective	Opposite
active	passive

3 | Language in use: Modern slavery

You are going to read a text about modern forms of slavery. Some words are missing from the text. Choose the correct answer (A, B, C or D) for each gap (1–11) in the text. Write your answers in the boxes provided. The first one (0) has been done for you.

The term slavery conjures up … **(0)** of the transatlantic slave trade that was abolished in the 19th century. However, according to the latest figures of the International Labour Organisation about 20 million people around the world are … **(Q1)** like slaves. These poor people are forced to work – either through physical or mental pressure, they are owned and closely controlled by their masters – often through mental or physical abuse or the … **(Q2)** of abuse, they are treated as a commodity that can be bought and sold, and finally they are restricted in their movements.

Modern slavery can … **(Q3)** people of all ages, gender and ethnic background. In many cases workers in developing countries are treated like slaves and have to work under … **(Q4)** conditions for minimal wages in order to produce goods which their masters can sell to Western companies for a fraction of what these companies earn in the Western world. And in spite of these low prices the company owners in developing countries still … **(Q5)** enormous amounts of money – at least for the countries they live in.

When a textile factory in Bangladesh … **(Q6)** on 24 April 2013, over 1,045 textile workers making clothes for Western brands were killed. This accident drew international … **(Q7)** to the plight of poor Bangladeshis who were held like slaves and forced to work without proper protection and … **(Q8)** regulations. As a consequence of this disaster new guidelines were drawn up to improve the situation of the … **(Q9)** in the garment factories in Bangladesh and elsewhere.

However, as long as consumers in Western countries keep buying clothes from major brands which sell goods produced under inhuman … **(Q10)** nothing will change in the developing world. The only way to put a … **(Q11)** to this development is to exert consumer power by refusing to buy textile products produced under such circumstances.

0	A	views	B	looks	C	images	D	portraits
Q1	A	threatened	B	treated	C	trodden	D	threaded
Q2	A	fright	B	treat	C	threat	D	fear
Q3	A	effect	B	affect	C	effectuate	D	afford
Q4	A	appealing	B	appalled	C	appealed	D	appalling
Q5	A	earn	B	have earned	C	had earned	D	put on
Q6	A	collided	B	colluded	C	collated	D	collapsed
Q7	A	excitement	B	attention	C	suspicion	D	focus
Q8	A	security	B	healthy	C	safety	D	safe
Q9	A	workforce	B	jobs	C	works	D	masters
Q10	A	circumstances	B	developments	C	reactions	D	atmosphere
Q11	A	finish	B	end	C	halt	D	stoppage

0	Q1	Q2	Q3	Q4	Q5	Q6	Q7	Q8	Q9	Q10	Q11
C ✓											

4 Language in use: HIV/AIDS in Hollywood movies

a) You are going to read a text about the representation of HIV/AIDS in Hollywood movies. Some words are missing from the text. Choose from the list (A–P) the correct part for each gap (1–13) in the text. There are two extra words you should not use. Write your answers in the boxes provided. The first one (0) has been done for you.

Hollywood has, since the … **(0)** of celluloid, played an important role in the … **(Q1)** of our society and people's ways of thinking. Often films allow us to open our minds and learn new things we may not have once understood or felt … **(Q2)** with.

But when I look back at the short and recent history of films that include HIV and/or AIDS in their plot, I find it … **(Q3)** to think of a single one that has challenged our way of thinking or … **(Q4)** our culture forward by bringing light to scenarios or situations that were true to today's way of living for those with HIV. One that … **(Q5)** the idea that having HIV is now manageable, and daily treatment with today's medications can, and most likely will, reduce your viral load, … **(Q6)** increasing the quality and length of your life.

The portrayals we've seen, while they may have been award-worthy, still pulled us further away from our goal of reducing … **(Q7)**. They may even have reinforced it. The huge absence of HIV-positive … **(Q8)** is not just limited to film. This is also true in … **(Q9)** TV. In fact the last non-reality US television series that included a main character living with HIV (and not dying of it) was Showtime's *Queer as Folk* – the finale aired in 2005. Between the … **(Q10)** of education that plagues our youth and the lack of … **(Q11)** among so-called low-risk populations, it's no wonder that stigma is the leading perpetrator of a … **(Q12)** infection rate year after year.

A large portion of the … **(Q13)** still doesn't know the difference between HIV and AIDS, and Hollywood has yet to come to the rescue.

(Scott McPherson, *thestigmaproject.org*, 1 November 2013; adapted and abridged)

A	advancement	**H**	losing	**O**	stigma	**0**	✓	**Q7**	
B	awareness	**I**	population	**P**	written	**Q1**		**Q8**	
C	comfortable	**J**	pushed			**Q2**		**Q9**	
D	consistent	**K**	reflects			**Q3**		**Q10**	
E	impossible	**L**	representation			**Q4**		**Q11**	
F	invention	**M**	scripted			**Q5**		**Q12**	
G	lack	**N**	significantly			**Q6**		**Q13**	

b) Study the text above and find synonyms for the phrases below.

1. views, attitudes: …*ways of thinking*………………………………………………………………………

2. to give us the opportunity: ……………………………………………………………………………………

3. drugs: ………

4. to be restricted to: ……………………………………………………………………………………………

5. to trouble: ………………………………………………………………………………………………………

6. mark of disgrace: ……………………………………………………………………………………………

5 Language in use: Tesla's next move

You are going to read a text about a company that produces electric cars. Some words are missing from the text. Use the words in brackets to complete each gap (1–14) in the text. Write your answers in the spaces provided at the end of the text. The first one (0) has been done for you.

It's a Thursday afternoon at the Tesla Factory in Fremont, California, and the robots are … **(0 hum)**. Humans in T-shirts and San Francisco Giants caps trade jokes as they help a massive … **(Q1 robot)** arm guide a touchscreen dashboard … **(Q2 assemble)** past the B-pillar of a partially built Model S. … **(Q3 Far)** down the assembly line, finished cars rest in sleek rows according to their export destinations: Frankfurt, Oslo, Hong Kong.

If Tesla's goal were simply to become a world-beating luxury automaker, crafting pricey toys for the … **(Q4 environment)** conscious elite, it would already have succeeded. But the aim of Elon Musk, one of the company's founders and current CEO, all along has been to build an electric car for the masses. … **(Q5 Specific)**, the company's plan is a $35,000 "third-generation" electric sedan with … **(Q6 compete)** performance and a 200-mile-plus range, all by the year 2017.

If Tesla pulls it off, it will secure its place among the world's great car companies while … **(Q7 help)** to push electric cars into the mainstream. If it doesn't, established players like Nissan and BMW will figure out the future of the car, electric or otherwise.

The … **(Q8 endure)** problem with electric cars is that batteries cost far more than internal combustion engines relative to the power they provide. Before Tesla, the … **(Q9 prevail)** approach was to keep electric cars as … **(Q10 afford)** as possible by skimping on … **(Q11 perform)** and range.

Musk turned that … **(Q12 calculate)** on its head by casting price concerns aside and building the best cars he could – the Model S costs $80,000, and it outperforms the best gas-guzzlers in its class.

It was a stroke of strategic … **(Q13 brilliant)**, but it didn't solve the underlying problem. Electric batteries are still nowhere near as cost-effective as gasoline engines (unless you count the societal costs of air … **(Q14 pollute)** – but that's another debate). Tesla is planning to solve this problem by building a huge battery factory. It will be the largest factory of its kind, capable of producing more lithium-ion batteries each year than were produced in the whole world in 2013. This will bring down the cost of its battery packs by more than 30 per cent.

(Will Oremus, *slate.com*, 14 May 2014; adapted and abridged)

0	*humming* ✔

Q1 ....

Q2 ....

Q3 ....

Q4 ....

Q5 ....

Q6 ....

Q7 ....

Q8 ....

Q9 ....

Q10 ....

Q11 ....

Q12 ....

Q13 ....

Q14 ....

6 Language in use: What is political correctness?

You are going to read a text about political correctness. In most lines of the text there is a word that should not be there. Write that word in the space provided after each line. Some lines are correct. Indicate these lines with a tick (✓). There are two examples at the beginning.

Political correctness is the result of a development **pattern** in society that	...pattern...	0
wants to promote equality and respect. The term political correctness	✓	00
in its present meaning way was first brought up by feminist and left-wing	....	Q1
movements in the US in the 1970s. Before the new term "politically	....	Q2
correct" was used to describe the way in which dictatorial regimes	....	Q3
prescribed the use of certain useful expressions to cover up what they	....	Q4
did not want to express openly only.	....	Q5
What PC means in effect is that people should change the way they	....	Q6
express themselves so that no other people, especially underprivileged	....	Q7
groups like women, ethnic minorities, etc. should hardly be offended.	....	Q8
In addition, PC wants to correct out political bias and tries to promote fair	....	Q9
and respectful behaviour.	....	Q10
Over the years politically correct language has become the object of	....	Q11
ridicule as it uses language patterns that do not represent themselves	....	Q12
what they are not supposed to express.	....	Q13
However noble the first promoters were, many people think that the	....	Q14
present focus on political correctness means taking things too far away.	....	Q15
What started out as a reaction to discrimination has not turned out to be	....	Q16
a language that is riddled with unusual and sometimes complicated	....	Q17
constructions which are sometimes hard to understand.	....	Q18
Political correctness is never extremely important in political discussions	....	Q19
and in the media. If you do not comply with the rules of PC you will	....	Q20
soon be stigmatised and – in many cases – excluded from the political	....	Q21
discourse level.	....	Q22

7 Paraphrasing

Rewrite these sentences in your own words. Use the words given.

1. The survey shows that the people in Europe are aware of the possible consequences of climate change. **(according to)**

   ...According to the survey the people...

2. In the opinion of many people politicians should do more to reduce carbon dioxide emissions quickly. **(think)**

   ....

3. The number of people who think that climate change is a serious problem has gone up in the last two years. **(rise)**

   ....

4. It would be better if political leaders did not underestimate the problem because that would be even worse. **(should)**

   ....

Lifelong learning

1 Expressing an opinion

a) Complete the quotes below with suitable words from the box. Make sure you use the correct forms (two of the verbs are used as nouns).

> to follow sb. • to graduate • to imitate sb. • ~~to know sth.~~ • to love sth. • to prepare for sth. • to stay young • to teach sb. • to unlearn sth.

"The more I live, the more I learn. The more I learn, the more I realise, the less I … **(1)**."
(Michel Legrand)

"The illiterate of the 21st century will not be those who cannot read and write, but those who cannot learn, … **(2)**, and relearn."
(Alvin Toffler)

"You'll never know everything about anything, especially something you … **(3)**."
(Julia Child)

"Education is not … **(4)** for life; education is life itself."
(John Dewey)

"Learning is a treasure that will … **(5)** its owner everywhere."
(Chinese Proverb)

"Anyone who stops learning is old, whether at twenty or eighty. Anyone who keeps learning … **(6)**."
(Henry Ford)

"The man who … **(7)** today and stops learning tomorrow is uneducated the day after."
(Newton D. Baker)

"By three methods we may learn wisdom: First, by reflection, which is the noblest; Second, by … **(8)**, which is the easiest; and third by experience, which is the bitterest."
(Confucius)

"I am always ready to learn although I do not always like being … **(9)**."
(Winston Churchill)

1. .... *know* ....
2. ....
3. ....
4. ....
5. ....
6. ....
7. ....
8. ....
9. ....

b) Voice your opinion on some of the quotes above by completing the following sentence starters.

1. As far as I'm concerned, ...

2. I completely agree with ....

3. As far as I understand it, ...

4. I'd like to point out that ....

5. It's unjustifiable to say that ....

6. I'm sorry to disagree with ....

7. It is generally accepted that ....

8. I'd go along with ....

9. Speaking for myself ....

10. I couldn't agree more with ....

2 Home schooling: If a child gets bored at school, blame the system

a) Do you associate the words below rather with the traditional education system or with home schooling, an educational model in which parents tutor their children at home?

> adventure • anti-bullying • attention span • coach • connection to life • creative •
> curious • curriculum • drama group • eagerness • excellence • excitement • facilities •
> fascination • frustration • idling • novelty • patience • repetitive • stimulating •
> timetable • tutor

Traditional education system	Home schooling

b) Fill in the opposites of the words below. Use the words from the blue box in task a.

Word	Opposite		Word	Opposite
1. disinterested	curious		5. active	
2. indifference			6. outdatedness	
3. disinterest			7. interesting	
4. triumph			8. dull	

c) You are going to read a text about home schooling. Some words are missing from the text. Fill in the word which best fits each gap (1–10). Use only one word in each gap. Write your answers in the spaces provided at the end of the text. The first one (0) has been done for you.

My daughter Matilda loved reading. She always asked … **(0)**. Her mind was a cauldron of bubbly eagerness, never idling, ever curious. That was ten years ago, when she was nearly seven, brimming with excitement about … **(Q1)** off into a new academic year at her school in Kent. But over the … **(Q2)** of that one term she turned into a completely different child. She stopped reading. Getting ready for school became a daily battle. It was as if her innate curiosity had flipped, like a … **(Q3)**, into angry, bitter complaint. Something had gone terribly wrong.

It dawned on me, gradually, that she was quite simply bored, not least because she was being given mind-numbingly repetitive work. Matilda's teacher insisted there wasn't a problem as she was doing well in her tests. The head teacher told us not to fuss, it was a phase that would soon pass. But seeing our fizz-ball of a daughter literally fizzle out within just a few weeks of changing class was too appalling for us to see. We felt compelled to do something. We tried … **(Q4)** for another school – both in the private and state sectors. To our astonishment, none offered us much comfort. They talked about wonderful food, superlative facilities, excellence in health and safety, anti-bullying and, of course, their great results, but none ever volunteered a zero-tolerance policy on boredom.

Initially, we … **(Q5)** to home educate for a year while we searched for a more creative, stimulating school for Matilda and her younger sister Verity. We created a schoolroom at home. We found a ready-made curriculum on the web and divided the day into a timetable. You can be relaxed about informing the authorities in the UK as, unlike in some other countries (e.g. Japan and Germany), there is no formal legal obligation to educate your children at a school or to follow the national … **(Q6)**. I led on science while my wife plunged into music, maths, history and English. We found a French tutor and a tennis coach, and the girls joined local dance and drama groups. I moved to a four-day working … **(Q7)** while my wife threw herself into home educating full time.

After the initial novelty of not going to school wore … **(Q8)** (it took perhaps a week) everyone's patience began to wear thin, frustration boiled over, attention spans shortened and, to cap it all, Matilda said she found it just like being at school but at home. In a word: boring. But we knew that for Matilda, the world was a wonderland of curiosity and fascination. We were desperate to find a way back to that place. And so … **(Q9)** reading books written by people with similar experiences, and a great deal of discussion, we tried something totally different, sat Matilda down and asked her, "Matilda – what are you interested in?" It sounds crazy, but – think about it – our educational system never asks that question. Rather it says that at 11:30 a.m. on Tuesdays you will do biology, and in term 2 of year 6 you will be doing photosynthesis. Why? Because it says so in the curriculum. There is no connection or relevance to the child's life. And her … **(Q10)** to our question? "PENGUINS!" What?! "I want to learn all about penguins." And so began our new educational adventure.

(Christopher Lloyd, *The Telegraph*, 2 September 2013; adapted and abridged)

0	*questions* ✔

Q1	....	Q6	....
Q2	....	Q7	....
Q3	....	Q8	....
Q4	....	Q9	....
Q5	....	Q10	....

d) Match the words taken from the text above with the correct definitions

1.	cauldron	F	A	sth. new or unusual
2.	to brim with sth.		B	to be or become upset or worried
3.	innate		C	courses that are taught by a school or college
4.	mind-numbing		D	commitment to do sth. because of a law or rule
5.	to fuss over sth.		E	very dull or boring
6.	curriculum		F	large pot
7.	obligation		G	to overflow, to bustle
8.	novelty		H	determined by factors present in an individual from birth

3 Taking a gap year

a) Which of the words and phrases below could you use to answer the following questions? Make mind maps to sort the items accordingly.

- *What is a gap year?*
- *Why do people take a gap year?*
- *When can a gap year be taken?*

- *Where can you go?*
- *What can you do?*
- *How could a gap year be organised?*

academic year · commitment · degree course · determination · enterprise · expedition · formal education · independent · internship · learning experiences · maturity · organisational skills · period of time · postgraduate course · self-motivation · structured gap package · travel company · travel destination · tuition fee · voluntary work

to encourage sb. to do sth. · to finish school · to go directly to university · to have/take a break · to look for adventure · to look good on the CV · to pay for accommodation · to pick up new skills · to save up for a trip · to see more of the world · to spend one's time · to start higher education · to take on a part-time job

b) Complete the sentences below with suitable words from above.

1. A "gap year" is a period of time, usually an ....*academic year*.........., when a student takes a break from formal education. It is often spent travelling or working.

2. In the past you took a gap year if you had to retake exams or had problems between .... and starting higher education and then starting a career.

3. Many universities .... students to take a gap year, and employers are happy to give jobs to students who have gained experience through a gap year.

4. A year out before moving on to higher education can give young people useful learning experiences, help them .... new skills and make them more independent.

5. Gap years can also be taken at a different time, for example, by someone who wants to break up their .... or to do something different before a postgraduate course.

6. A lot of gap year students choose to do .... This could include teaching in Nepal, taking part in a conservation project in Ghana, or helping to rebuild a village in Chile.

7. Popular gap year activities for young people .... include surfing in Hawaii, wakeboarding in Italy, kitesurfing in Egypt or bungee jumping in New Zealand.

8. Many gap year students just want to .... According to a British survey, the top five travel destinations for 2013 were Tibet, Indonesia, Taiwan, Eastern Europe and Canada.

9. Most students who are planning a gap year take on a part-time job to .... for the trip.

10. Because the gap year is so popular and needs to be cheap, travel companies now offer structured .... where your entire trip is worked out for you.

c) Write short paragraphs on the six questions from task a. Use the words and phrases from this section.

4 Language in use: Applying for university

a) *You are going to read an extract from an application letter to a university. In most lines of the text there is a word that should not be there. Write that word in the space provided after each line. Some lines are correct. Indicate these lines with a tick (✓). There are two examples at the beginning.*

I am writing to express my interest **rate** in studying at the University of	*rate*	0
South Carolina. I am currently completing my last **of** semester in Chinook	*of*	00
High School, and I will be graduating in two weeks. I have always found		Q1
the field of education to be fascinating and both rewarding. Thus, a		Q2
bachelor's degree in education has been my dream. I have spent my		Q3
high school years in Ohio. Although I feel that I have acquired a solid		Q4
intellectual foundation to continue pursuing after my under-graduate		Q5
studies at the University of South Carolina as proved by the enclosed		Q6
SAT score and my GPA. I have also received several honours and		Q7
awards ceremonies for my academic achievement during the middle		Q8
and high school years book. In addition, I have acquired transferable		Q9
skills such as the ability to identify and solve the problems, excellent		Q10
verbal and written communication skills, and an appreciation for		Q11
attention to detail that will continue helping me do well being and		Q12
succeed in my future professional life. More importantly, I am highly		Q13
motivated. I will understand that qualities such as patience, diligence,		Q14
sensitivity, enthusiasm and commitment are not needed in order to work		Q15
with children in the school and extra-curricular setting and neither I		Q16
believe I would prove a valuable asset to the educational field trip. As		Q17
required by the school, I am enclosing the filled-in application form		Q18
to pursue my bachelor's degree in education from your esteemed school.		Q19
In addition, my resume and three complaint letters of recommendation		Q20
are attached here.		Q21

b) *Complete the sentences below with suitable words. Make sure you use the correct forms.*

academic achievement   application form   to be highly motivated

~~to express one's interest in sth.~~   to graduate

solid intellectual foundation   transferable skills

1. I am writing to ....*express my interest in*.... studying at the University of South Carolina.
2. I am currently completing my last semester in Chinook High School, and I .... in two weeks.
3. I feel that I have acquired a .... to continue pursuing my undergraduate studies at the University of South Carolina as proved by the enclosed SAT score and my GPA.
4. I have also received several honours and awards for my .... during the middle and high school years.
5. I have acquired .... such as the ability to identify and solve problems, excellent verbal and written communication skills, and an appreciation for attention to detail.
6. I am .... and am a student with good academic, athletic and interpersonal skills.
7. As required by the school, I am enclosing the filled-in .... to pursue my bachelor's degree in education from your esteemed school.

Sample Matura tasks

1 Multiple choice: Migrants in Mexico waiting to cross

You are going to read a text about a migrants waiting to cross the border to the US. Some words are missing from the text. Choose the correct answer (A, B, C or D) for each gap (1–9) in the text. Write your answers in the boxes provided. The first one (0) has been done for you.

If it … **(0)** live off legitimate enterprise, Altar, in Sonora state, would be just another victim of the battering Mexico's rural economy has suffered. But the tiny town … **(Q1)** in a way that its vanished ranchers could not have imagined. The thousands of young people who … **(Q2)** into town every month are the raw material of its new industry: immigrant smuggling.

Located just 60 miles south of Arizona, Altar … **(Q3)** as a giant waiting room for migrants crossing into America through one of the most punishing deserts in the western hemisphere. "It's the last piece of civilisation they'll see for three, four, five or six days," says Francisco Garcia Aten, who manages a shelter … **(Q4)** by the Catholic church.

Founded as a military base in 1775, the town lost its farm income during an economic crisis in the 1990s. At the same time, American immigration authorities tightened the border in urban areas, pushing migrants into remote areas like southern Arizona. In cooler weather, some 1,000 to 3,000 a day … **(Q5)** in Altar, whose resident population is just 14,000.

On any street corner they can … **(Q6)** buying backpacks, water, shoes, hats and tinned food especially in the cooler spring months. A ride to the border, with 25–30 migrants crammed into a van, costs $15. From there prices vary, depending on how far the "coyotes" take their … **(Q7)**.

The lucky ones soon find themselves picking grapes in California or roofing houses in Florida. Many … **(Q8)**, deported or both, often ending up back in Altar. One man … **(Q9)** 28 times before making it into the United States, says Mr Garcia.

(The Economist, 10 August 2006; adapted and abridged)

0	A	have to	B	is able to	∅	had to	D	can
Q1	A	booms	B	is booming	C	boomed	D	has boomed
Q2	A	peer	B	pear	C	pour	D	pair
Q3	A	has served	B	served	C	serves	D	is served
Q4	A	provided	B	providing	C	proved	D	proving
Q5	A	have arrived	B	will arrive	C	arrived	D	arrive
Q6	A	spot	B	be seen	C	observe	D	see
Q7	A	consumers	B	costumers	C	customers	D	custodians
Q8	A	rob	B	are robbing	C	are robbed	D	robbers
Q9	A	has tried	B	tried	C	is tried	D	is trying

0	Q1	Q2	Q3	Q4	Q5	Q6	Q7	Q8	Q9
C ✔									

2 Banked gap fill: Sport paves the way

You are going to read a text about sports and scholarships. Some words are missing from the text. Choose from the list (A–R) the correct part for each gap (1–15) in the text. There are two extra words you should not use. Write your answers in the boxes provided. The first one (0) has been done for you.

Going to … **(0)** in the US is a … **(Q1)** investment for students and their families. It pays off, however, because the job … **(Q2)** for college graduates are much better and the pay is … **(Q3)** higher than for the average school … **(Q4)**.

As a result, more and more young people are faced with the … **(Q5)** that they have the intellectual talents to move on to college but their financial … **(Q6)** would not allow them to study for several years without … **(Q7)** income. For many the way out is to join a sports team and do sports … **(Q8)** in order to be eligible for a scholarship at a university. This may be the track-and-field team, a baseball team or the rugby squad – the important thing is to stand out and be … **(Q9)** by the talent scouts of university and college teams.

A recent … **(Q10)** in this area is rugby which is … **(Q11)** as prestigious which means that colleges recruit players as young as 13. There is a growing number of teenagers often from underprivileged backgrounds who see rugby and fringe sports in general as an … **(Q12)** route into college. If the young … **(Q13)** are good enough they may even have the choice between … **(Q14)** from various universities and colleges. So the message to teenagers who … **(Q15)** to go to college is join a sports team and work your way up to the top.

A	alternative	**I**	further	**Q**	tendency	**0**	E ✓	**Q8**
B	aspire	**J**	leaver	**R**	trend	**Q1**		**Q9**
C	athletes	**K**	major			**Q2**		**Q10**
D	background	**L**	prospects			**Q3**		**Q11**
E	college	**M**	realised			**Q4**		**Q12**
F	competitively	**N**	recognised			**Q5**		**Q13**
G	considerably	**O**	regarded			**Q6**		**Q14**
H	dilemma	**P**	scholarships			**Q7**		**Q15**

3 Open gap fill: Paper cups

You are going to read a text about paper cups and their history. Some words are missing from the text. Fill in the word which best fits each gap (1–8). Use only one word in each gap. Write your answers in the spaces provided at the end of the text. The first one (0) has been done for you.

When we think of paper cups we get the impression that they are fairly … **(0)**. They seem to have been introduced with American … **(Q1)** chains. However, paper cups were already used in China as early as the 2nd century BC.

The modern paper cup became … **(Q2)** at the beginning of the 20th century because of health … **(Q3)**. Paper cups were mainly used instead of glasses in public places, e.g. in schools or on trains, to give people the chance to drink water from a tap.

Paper cups are made of special paper, which needs to be waterproof and stiff to make the cups easy to handle. Clay was first … **(Q4)** to make cups waterproof, but soon it was … **(Q5)** by wax and nowadays paper cups are coated with a thin layer of polyethylene.

As paper cups are usually … **(Q6)** for single use only, they contribute considerably to household waste. And if they … **(Q7)** up on landfill sites, they do not degrade quickly. The latest development is cups coated with biodegradable … **(Q8)** which makes them easier to compost.

0	new ✔

Q1	....
Q2	....
Q3	....
Q4	....

Q5	....
Q6	....
Q7	....
Q8	....

4 Editing: Gennaro Contaldo – Jamie Oliver's mentor

You are going to read a text about the famous master chef Gennaro Contaldo. In most lines of the text there is a word that should not be there. Write that word in the space provided after each line. Some lines are correct. Indicate these lines with a tick (✓). There are two examples at the beginning.

Being a master chef these days is not just preparing fancy **dress** dishes for	...dress... **0**
others and running an expensive restaurant. It is more like being a media	✔ **00**
star with all the highs and lows that come along with the limelight. But getting	.... **Q1**
to the top is not as easy as it seems. Gennaro Contaldo was born in Italy where	.... **Q2**
he grew up in a small village under on the Amalfi Coast. It was this rural	.... **Q3**
upbringing that helped him develop a taste for the natural, unspoilt	.... **Q4**
ingredients and simple dishes. His interest in food and cooking was often	.... **Q5**
fostered in this environment, so much so that at the age of eight he started	.... **Q6**
working in his local restaurants laying the basis for his further career.	.... **Q7**
Later in London, he worked for famous restaurants, among them Carluccio's in	.... **Q8**
the Convent Garden, before he opened his own and became famous. One of	.... **Q9**
the many people he worked with was a young Jamie Oliver, whose mentor he	.... **Q10**
became. Together they were started various projects, among them "Fifteen",	.... **Q11**
Jamie Oliver's restaurant which offers a career of path for young unemployed	.... **Q12**
people to give them the only chance of a better future, which became a true	.... **Q13**
success story.	.... **Q14**

5 Word formation: Alcoholics Anonymous

You are going to read a text about alcoholism. Some words are missing from the text. Use the words in brackets to complete each gap (1–12) in the text. Write your answers in the spaces provided at the end of the text. The first one (0) has been done for you.

Alcoholics anonymous is an … (**0 organise**) whose members try to help each other to battle alcoholism by sharing their experiences and their hopes to recover from what is regarded as an … (**Q1 ill**).

If you want to join them you have to be willing to stop drinking alcohol. There are no … (**Q2 enter**) fees or other membership … (**Q3 regulate**). Moreover, AA is not affiliated with any religious or … (**Q4 politics**) group or other institution. Its sole intention is to provide support, but it does not engage in controversies. Its main objective is for its members to stay sober and to help others to do the same.

In many cases they have to deal with people who drown their daily … (**Q5 frustrate**) in alcohol. Or they drink simply because they cannot stand the … (**Q6 press**) at home or in the work place. For many, however, the most difficult step is to admit that they have a drinking problem. Very often people … (**Q7 suffer**) from alcohol abuse hide their problems from themselves as well as from others. At the same time, they feel bad about what they are doing and this leads to further alcohol … (**Q8 abusive**).

But how can you find out if you are in danger of becoming … (**Q9 addict**) to alcohol? You can ask yourself if you think about drinking before going out or before going home in the evening. Or do you feel … (**Q10 easy**) when the topic is raised in a conversation? Have you ever had blackouts after a night at a party? These may be the first … (**Q11 indicate**) that you should have a … (**Q12 close**) look at your lifestyle and maybe look for help.

0	*organisation* ✔

Q1	....	Q7	....
Q2	....	Q8	....
Q3	....	Q9	....
Q4	....	Q10	....
Q5	....	Q11	....
Q6	....	Q12	....

6 Multiple choice: Is queuing really the British way?

You are going to read a text about queuing. Some words are missing from the text. Choose the correct answer (A, B, C or D) for each gap (1–9) in the text. Write your answers in the boxes provided. The first one (0) has been done for you.

Queuing, it's what the British are famous for doing – and doing very well. It even has its own code of conduct in … **(0)**, heaven forbid, anyone doesn't understand how the queue works. Yet queuing in a calm, good-natured manner has not always come naturally. "We're … **(Q1)** to be so wonderful at it but really that reputation is built around a whole mythology," says Dr Joe Moran, a social historian.

The temporary nature of queues makes it hard to … **(Q2)** their history, but key historical events are said to have shaped how the British queue. One is the industrial revolution. "The orderly queue seems to have developed in the early 19th century, a product of more urbanised societies which brought … **(Q3)** of people together," says Moran. People were moving in huge numbers into towns changing the patterns of daily life, including shopping. "The whole way people shopped was more informal," says historian Juliet Gardiner. "Traders started moving from market … **(Q4)** into shops as they moved into towns. In the more formal setting of a shop people had to start to queue up in a more structured way."

Despite the mass expansion of manufacturing not everyone did well and many people were poor. "Thus queuing started to become … **(Q5)** with extreme hardship as the poor had to queue to access handouts and charity," says Dr Kate Bradley, a lecturer in social history at the University of Kent.

But what really shaped Britain's reputation as civilised queuers was World War II. "Propaganda at the time was all about doing your duty and … **(Q6)** your turn," says Bradley. "It was a way the government tried to control a situation in uncertain times." The queue became loaded with meaning, and the myth of the British as patient queuers was forged, says Moran. "In reality there were arguments, and often the police had to be brought in to … **(Q7)** things out. Queuing was exhausting and frustrating. Things would go on sale in an erratic way, and people often … **(Q8)** the end of a queue without knowing exactly what it was for, they just hoped it would be something useful."

The notion of the orderly queue is a belief that is still cherished today. "It's a story we still like to tell about ourselves," says Moran. "We like to think it … **(Q9)** in with a particular idea we have of our national character – that we're pragmatic and phlegmatic."

(Denise Winterman, *BBC News Magazine*, 4 July 2013; adapted and abridged)

0	A	situation	B	spite	C	case	D	supposing
Q1	A	likely	B	so-called	C	counted	D	supposed
Q2	A	charge	B	define	C	draw	D	trace
Q3	A	mobs	B	volumes	C	masses	D	piles
Q4	A	houses	B	stalls	C	auctions	D	sales
Q5	A	isolated	B	associated	C	regarded	D	thought
Q6	A	waiting	B	queuing	C	standing	D	making
Q7	A	sort	B	make	C	try	D	move
Q8	A	came	B	waited	C	joined	D	added
Q9	A	fits	B	comes	C	believes	D	proves

0	Q1	Q2	Q3	Q4	Q5	Q6	Q7	Q8	Q9
C ✓									

7 Banked gap fill: What's proper social media etiquette at a celebrity wedding?

You are going to read a text about how to use social media at celebrity weddings. Some words are missing from the text. Choose from the list (A–L) the correct part for each gap (1–9) in the text. There are two extra words you should not use. Write your answers in the boxes provided. The first one (0) has been done for you.

Although the Kardashian-Jenner clan has been instagramming up a storm in the days leading up to the Kimye wedding, they will probably slow to a … **(0)** once the nuptials begin. Kim Kardashian and Kanye West will likely … **(Q1)** cell phones and social media at their ceremony. And while we're bummed that we won't witness the festivities in … **(Q2)** time, it's no surprise since the list of celebrities who are prohibiting social media is ever-growing. Last week, Poppy Delevingne asked guests not to post anything from her wedding to James Cook to social media, and couples like Blake Lively and Ryan Reynolds have … **(Q3)** to keep their marriages secret for some time by doing the same.

In an age where everything is instant, banning social media from your wedding can be a good way to control what gets out there, even if you don't have millions of people clamouring to see your dress. According to David's Bridal's eighth annual "What's on Brides' Minds" survey, 44 per cent of brides believe that having rules when it comes to your wedding and social media is … **(Q4)**. However, only 14 per cent are banning social media altogether.

On the other end of the … **(Q5)**, many brides are creating social media hashtags and … **(Q6)** guests to post. Twenty-six per cent of respondents said they want guests to use their special wedding hashtag. During her New Year's Eve wedding, Kaley Cuoco … **(Q7)** photos throughout the night and created a hashtag for guests to post to. However, 58 per cent of brides believe that the bride and groom should be the first ones to share photos of the wedding. That's exactly what Chrissy Teigen did when she married John Legend last September. … **(Q8)** there were no photos on Instagram or Twitter during the actual wedding, Teigen posted a photo after the fact.

But what is the biggest social media no-no? Bridesmaids posting photos of the bride in her dress before the … **(Q9)** sees her. Sixty-two per cent of respondents said no pictures of the bride should be shared before the ceremony. How's that for old-fashioned?

(Rita Kokshanian, *InStyle.com*, 23 May 2014; adapted and abridged)

A	affront	**F**	important	**K**	spectrum	**0**	L (✓)	**Q5**
B	although	**G**	managed	**L**	standstill	**Q1**		**Q6**
C	ban	**H**	real			**Q2**		**Q7**
D	encourage	**I**	secret			**Q3**		**Q8**
E	groom	**J**	shared			**Q4**		**Q9**

8 Open gap fill: Project helps parents to help their children

You are going to read a text about a school project in Wales. Some words are missing from the text. Fill in the word which best fits each gap (1–10). Use only one word in each gap. Write your answers in the spaces provided at the end of the text. The first one (0) has been done for you.

For those of us who … (0) our way through the Welsh education system before the year 2000, or even that of five or ten years … (Q1), our experiences will inevitably be different from those of the current generation of school children, who are in the middle of a Welsh government drive to boost … (Q2) standards in literacy and numeracy.

You might think the most fundamental difference is that this generation have never known a time … (Q3) the internet, smart phones or tablets. But with so … (Q4) incremental government changes to our education system in recent years and current plans to develop a unique curriculum specifically for Wales, the way in which core … (Q5) like maths and English are taught now will inevitably be different … (Q6) the way the previous generation (or two, or three) were taught. Equally, some of the content in today's syllabus may not have been taught in the past – which means parents or carers couldn't help … (Q7) if they wanted to.

This is where schools are … (Q8) steps to encourage parents and carers to come along to after-school sessions and community events, to help them to engage not only in school life but the very things their children are learning on the curriculum. Of course, trying to balance work, family and after-school sessions is far from easy, especially if you don't live near your child's school. This is why sessions like those organised by Newport's Duffryn High School … (Q9) place every Wednesday in the community itself, at the old library in Pill where many students and their families live.

"In the evenings we go over how you can work with your child in English and maths, the heads of English and maths show them what the course is and what the demands will be, and simple techniques of … (Q10) they can help their child," explained Duffryn head teacher Jon Wilson, whose school was recently praised by the education inspectorate for its high percentage of "good" or "excellent" lessons.

(South Wales Argus, 21 May 2014; adapted and abridged)

0	*made* ✔

Q1 ....

Q2 ....

Q3 ....

Q4 ....

Q5 ....

Q6 ....

Q7 ....

Q8 ....

Q9 ....

Q10 ....

9 Editing: As lovely as a tree? Poem in UK cleanses air pollution

You are going to read a text about an art and environmental project in the UK. In most lines of the text there is a word that should not be there. Write that word in the space provided after each line. Some lines are correct. Indicate these lines with a tick (✓). There are two examples at the beginning.

Those towering billboards and advertisements may soon be **like** more than	*like*	0
just plain eye-catchers against a backdrop of blue skies and skyscrapers. In a	✓	00
matter of years, they could neither be the solution for the escalating problem	....	Q1
of air pollution, and it all begins with a poem in solely dedicated to one of	....	Q2
human's sources of life insurance. The poem, fittingly titled "In Praise of Air",	....	Q3
was written by an award-winning British poet, playwright and novelist Simon	....	Q4
Armitage. What sets it apart from all the usual printed-out literary work is	....	Q5
that it literally purifies the air. How does it work? The other material used to	....	Q6
carry the 122-word poem is made from a unique formula one that was	....	Q7
developed at the University of Sheffield. It is coated with chemical substances	....	Q8
recognised of being able to cut air pollution significantly by using sunlight and	....	Q9
oxygen masks, hence cleansing the air. The 10-metre by 20-metre piece of	....	Q10
material on which the poem was not printed can eliminate the same	....	Q11
amount of the toxic nitrogen oxide produced by roughly 20 cars in Britain	....	Q12
across each day. The technology is inexpensive, adding about only less	....	Q13
than £100 in each ad that would be using it. It could be included in every	....	Q14
flag store, banner or advertisement alongside busy roads and thereby	....	Q15
help Britain by meet its air quality target in one easy step. "This is a fun	....	Q16
collaboration between science and the arts to highlight about the very serious	....	Q17
issue of poor air quality in our towns and cities," said professor Tony Ryan,	....	Q18
whether the University's Pro-Vice-Chancellor for Science. "The science behind	....	Q19
this is behind an additive which delivers a real environmental benefit that	....	Q20
could actually help cut disease and save lives."	....	Q21

(Cez Verzosa, *Tech Times*, 21 May 2014; adapted and abridged)

10 Word formation: Does folk art include your nan's knitting?

You are going to read text about an art exhibition in London. Some words are missing from the text. Use the words in brackets to complete each gap (1–12) in the text. Write your answers in the spaces provided at the end of the text. The first one (0) has been done for you.

One of the glories of Tate Britain's new summer show is a single, massive leather boot, nearly 3 foot long and officially … **(0 size)** at 74. It looks exactly like something a giant would wear. The first question is – why does such a smart giant need only one boot? And the second one is, what is it doing here anyway? This is Tate Britain and not Tate Modern, so hardly the obvious home for … **(Q1 concept)** art.

Even when you learn that the title of this summer's … **(Q2 exhibit)** is British Folk Art, the monstrous boot doesn't make immediate sense. "Folk art", if it conjures anything more than blank stares, is assumed to denote samplers, corn dollies and quilts, the … **(Q3 produce)** of an emphatically rural culture. This boot by contrast hung outside a Northampton cobbler for decades, a sign to the unlettered that here was a place to get your footwear fixed. In the Tate's exhibition it sits alongside other stuff from the … **(Q4 industry)** world: pub signs, funny jugs, ships' figureheads, all made by artisans and workers who may be accounted at least semi-skilled.

"We decided to back away from providing … **(Q5 define)** of folk art" explains co-curator Martin Myrone. Myrone and his colleagues Ruth Kenny and Jeff McMillan embarked on a country-wide rummage in museum vaults for objects that had already been … **(Q6 label)** as "folk" by local curators. In practice, this often meant items that had … **(Q7 arrival)** decades earlier and that no one had ever quite known what to do with: a sporting print or a weather vane.

The borders between high and low, art and artefact, have been troubled and troubling ever since people started … **(Q8 choice)** what to hang on their walls. When the Royal Academy was established in 1769, it made a point of … **(Q9 declaration)** that "no needlework, artificial flowers, cut paper, shell work or any such baubles should be … **(Q10 admit)**" within its elite precincts. No place, then, for the work of Mary Linwood, the 18th-century needleworker whose embroidered pictures feature in the Tate's exhibition. Linwood, from Leicester, made a fortune out of her "needle paintings" of well-known contemporary works by Reynolds, Gainsborough and Stubbs.

Looked at afresh, Linwood's work is somewhere between the downright ugly and the slyly smart. You could easily mistake her pictures for a clever … **(Q11 investigate)** into what happens when high-art images, such as Rembrandt's *Mother* or Gainsborough's *The Woodman* mutate into the lower status medium of embroidery. … **(Q12 alternative)**, you might just as easily stumble across them when clearing out your late great aunt's bungalow.

(Kathryn Hughes, *The Guardian*, 23 May 2014; adapted and abridged)

0	sized ✔

Q1 ....

Q2 ....

Q3 ....

Q4 ....

Q5 ....

Q6 ....

Q7 ....

Q8 ....

Q9 ....

Q10 ....

Q11 ....

Q12 ....

girls, **12.** go on, **13.** wait for, **14.** break up, **15.** catch on, **16.** be up, **17.** go for, **18.** be around

c) **1.** turn out: Seite 52, Zeile 2
   2. get up: Seite 52, Zeile 15
   3. go off: Seite 52, Zeile 35
   4. build up: Seite 52, Zeile 53
   5. come up to: Seite 52, Zeile 57
   6. call for: Seite 53, Zeile 3
   7. take out: Seite 53, Zeile 3
   8. come out with: Seite 53, Zeile 33
   9. meant for: Seite 54, Zeile 50
   10. happen to: Seite 54, Zeile 93
   11. go out with boys/girls: Seite 54, Zeile 99
   12. go on: Seite 54, Zeile 1
   13. wait for: Seite 54, Zeile 22
   14. break up: Seite 55, Zeile 42
   15. catch on: Seite 55, Zeile 44
   16. be up: Seite 55, Zeile 46
   17. go for: Seite 55, Zeile 66
   18. be around: Seite 55, Zeile 70

5 Mixed Conditionals 1: Difficult teenage years

1. remembered, **2.** want, **3.** realise, **4.** want, **5.** stopped, **6.** argued, **7.** would be, **8.** should they do, **9.** happens, **10.** would have had

6 Mixed conditionals 2

1. had met, **2.** had been stolen, **3.** would know, **4.** had spoken, **5.** had ordered, **6.** had found

Unit 5 Extreme situations (Key)

1 Extreme word wheel

b) Individuelle Schüler/innenantworten
d) **1.** operating theatres, **2.** agony/intensity, **3.** graduation, **4.** Cemetery, **5.** ice climbing

2 Language in use: Too much school stress may make kids sick

0: D, **Q1:** A, **Q2:** D, **Q3:** B, **Q4:** C, **Q5:** C, **Q6:** D, **Q7:** C, **Q8:** A, **Q9:** B, **Q10:** B

3 Conditions

Beispielantwort

1. If the note had been found earlier, he could have been rescued.
2. If he hadn't eaten the seeds, he could have survived.
3. If he hadn't added the wild potato plant, he might have starved due to a caloric deficit. Unfortunately he didn't know that this plant contains a toxic agent.

4. If ODAP is ingested, it brings about paralysis by over-stimulating nerve receptors.
5. If you consumed food containing ODAP occasionally, it wouldn't hurt you because as one component of an otherwise balanced diet it bears no risk of toxicity for a healthy person.
6. If the guidebook had warned him, he probably would have survived and would be in his mid-forties now.

4 Comparisons

1. When Christopher McCandless was found, he weighed less than a healthy person of his age.
2. Jon Krakauer speculated that eating wild potato seeds made McCandless weaker from day to day.
3. People believe that the wild potato plant is safer than any other vegetable.
4. Maybe Ronald Hamilton did more careful research than other investigators in McCandless's death.
5. According to Hamilton the wild potato plant was the most important cause for McCandless's death.
6. ODAP is more dangerous than many other types of poison.
7. Weak and stressed people are more threatened by ODAP than people with a balanced diet.

5 Language in use: My parents chose my husband

0: advice, **00:** ✓, **Q1:** the, **Q2:** ✓, **Q3:** popular, **Q4:** centre, **Q5:** did, **Q6:** to, **Q7:** which, **Q8:** ✓, **Q9:** detector, **Q10:** a, **Q11:** with, **Q12:** left, **Q13:** ✓, **Q14:** test, **Q15:** brother, **Q16:** ✓, **Q17:** with, **Q18:** ✓, **Q19:** fruit, **Q20:** for, **Q21:** tree

Unit 6 India (Key)

1 Finding useful expressions: India

British legacy, raw materials, nonviolent resistance, civil disobedience, population density, trading company, trade monopoly, official language, driving force, legislative assembly, central government

2 Finding the right meaning

1. F, **2.** D, **3.** H, **4.** G, **5.** I, **6.** A, **7.** E, **8.** B, **9.** J, **10.** C

3 Language in use: Connectives – Elections in India

0: C, **Q1:** B, **Q2:** C, **Q3:** A, **Q4:** A, **Q5:** D, **Q6:** B, **Q7:** B, **Q8:** C, **Q9:** A, **Q10:** C

4 Language in use: The caste system

0: spiritual
Q1: development
Q2: closely

Q3: rulers
Q4: traders
Q5: labourers
Q6: ranking
Q7: rules
Q8: punishment
Q9: strengthen
Q10: unacceptable
Q11: unsuccessful
Q12: adoption
Q13: economic
Q14: addition
Q15: Gradually
Q16: divisions

5 Language in use: Mohandas Karamchand Gandhi – The Great Soul

0: K, **Q1:** D, **Q2:** F, **Q3:** G, **Q4:** L, **Q5:** N, **Q6:** E, **Q7:** C, **Q8:** M, **Q9:** B, **Q10:** J, **Q11:** H; **Not used:** activation (A), movement (I)

6 Synonyms and antonyms

1. independent, **2.** discrimination, **3.** strategy, **4.** supporters, **5.** taxes, **6.** creation, **7.** to split, **8.** territories

7 Language in use: Bollywood

0: combination
Q1: originated
Q2: growing
Q3: released
Q4: sold
Q5: financially
Q6: entertainment
Q7: popular
Q8: Originally
Q9: colourful
Q10: specifically
Q11: typical
Q12: following

Unit 7 Celebrities (Key)

1 Too many talent shows on TV in China?

a–b) 1. copycat (+), **2.** opportunities (–),
3. broadcasting (?), **4.** choice (+), **5.** audience's (+),
6. unpopular (–), **7.** uncover (–), **8.** standards (–),
9. ratings (?), **10.** excellent (–), **11.** thrive (–),
12. administrative (–), **13.** improve (–)
c) Individuelle Schüler/innenantworten

2 Language in use: How to know all the latest celebrity gossip

0: unexpectedly
Q1: disadvantage
Q2: unrealistic
Q3: insignificant
Q4: irresistible
Q5: unwilling
Q6: misleading
Q7: nonstop
Q8: Unlike
Q9: uncensored
Q10: distasteful
Q11: inappropriate
Q12: inconvenient
Q13: mis-/disinformed
Q14: impatient
Q15: unhappy
Q16: illegal

3 Opposites, opposites

a) un-: unable, unafraid, unavailable, unaware, uncertain, unclear, unfriendly, unhelpful, unknown, unpleasant, unrealistic
de-/dis-: to deactivate, to disagree, to deconstruct, to disinform, disloyal, displeased, to distrust
im-/in-: inaccurate, inadequate, inappropriate, incapable, incompatible, incomplete, inflexible, immature, impatient, imperfect, impossible, insecure, insignificant, insufficient, invisible
ir-: irregular, irrelevant, irresistible, irresponsible
il-: illegal, illegible, illiterate, illogical
b) 1. unable, **2.** illegal, **3.** unafraid, **4.** insufficient, **5.** deactivate, **6.** illiterate, **7.** inappropriate, **8.** distrust, **9.** uncertain, **10.** impatient

4 Learning vocabulary: Recording vocabulary

a) 1. close-up, **2.** extra, **3.** cutter, **4.** cast, **5.** director, **6.** credits, **7.** screenplay, **8.** location
b)–c) Individuelle Schüler/innenantworten

5 Language in use: Attack of the paparazzi

0: actually
Q1: hundreds
Q2: makes
Q3: consumers
Q4: tiniest
Q5: awareness
Q6: sixth
Q7: alarming
Q8: finally
Q9: security
Q10: constantly
Q11: different
Q12: neighbourhood

Unit 8 Art (Key)

1 Artists

Performing arts and music: actor/actress, ballet dancer, choreographer, composer, conductor, director, DJ, entertainer, musician, singer, soloist , vocalist
Visual arts: cartoonist , designer, graphic designer, illustrator , painter , sculptor, VJ
Literature: author, dramatist, lyricist, novelist, playwright, poet , scriptwriter, songwriter, storyteller, writer

2 Finding the right meaning

1. I, **2.** E, **3.** J, **4.** N, **5.** A, **6.** M, **7.** B, **8.** C, **9.** F, **10.** G, **11.** D, **12.** H, **13.** K, **14.** L

3 Language in use: What the artist says

0: C, **Q1:** B, **Q2:** B, **Q3:** A, **Q4:** D, **Q5:** B, **Q6:** A, **Q7:** C, **Q8:** B, **Q9:** C, **Q10:** B, **Q11:** C, **Q12:** D, **Q13:** C, **Q14:** D, **Q15:** B, **Q16:** A, **Q17:** C, **Q18:** B

4 Language in use: The Guggenheim Museum Bilbao

0: greatest
Q1: undoubtedly/doubtlessly
Q2: Situated
Q3: considerably
Q4: industrialism
Q5: investment
Q6: construction
Q7: cooperation
Q8: spectacular
Q9: exhibition
Q10: spanning
Q11: artists
Q12: opening
Q13: dominant/dominating
Q14: attraction

5 Language in use: Confusable words – Abstract art

0: C, **Q1:** C, **Q2:** B, **Q3:** C, **Q4:** B, **Q5:** D, **Q6:** A, **Q7:** A, **Q8:** D, **Q9:** A, **Q10:** B, **Q11:** C, **Q12:** C, **Q13:** D

Unit 9 Ethnic and cultural diversity (Key)

1 Bias and stereotyping

a) **Age:** 1, 3, 7
   Culture: 2, 4, 12
   Gender: 5, 8, 9, 10
   Other: 6, 11

b) **1.** Absolutely all, **2.** Virtually every, **3.** frequently, **4.** always, **5.** Generally speaking, **6.** Basically, **7.** normal, **8.** Most, **9.** almost never, **10.** usually, **11.** definitely, **12.** There's no doubt
c)–d): Individuelle Schüler/innenantworten

2 Racial (in)equality

a) **1.** covert, **2.** unintentional, **3.** state, **4.** self-righteous/blatant, **5.** scientific, **6.** institutional, **7.** interminority, **8.** blatant/self-righteous
b) **1.** minority group, **2.** tolerance, **3.** discrimination, **4.** immigration, **5.** favourite, **6.** segregation, **7.** uniformity
c) **1.** blatant, **2.** diversity, **3.** majority, **4.** institutional, **5.** scapegoats, **6.** segregation, **7.** affirmative action, **8.** Covert, **9.** emigration, **10.** discrimination
d) Individuelle Schüler/innenantworten

3 Language in use: Diwali – The festival of lights

0: with
Q1: evil
Q2: stands
Q3: cleaning
Q4: up
Q5: fuelled
Q6: way
Q7: against
Q8: date
Q9: start
Q10: which
Q11: become
Q12: before

4 The history of Ellis Island

a) **For over 60 years**, Ellis Island was the gateway for millions of immigrants to the United States. **From 1892 to 1924**, it was America's largest and most active immigration station, where over twelve million immigrants were processed.

It has been estimated that close to 40 per cent of all current US citizens can trace at least one of their ancestors back to Ellis Island. On average, the inspection process took approximately three to seven hours. For the vast majority of immigrants, Ellis Island was an "Island of Hope" – the first stop on their way to new opportunities and experiences in America. For some, though, it became the "Island of Tears" – a place where families were separated and individuals were denied entry into the country.

Ellis Island opened to the public **in 1976**. Today, visitors can tour the Ellis Island Immigration Museum in the restored Main

Arrivals Hall and trace their ancestors through millions of immigrant arrival records made available to the public **in 2001**. In this way, Ellis Island remains a central destination for millions of Americans seeking a glimpse into the past of their country, and, in many cases, into their own family's history.

b) **1.** opened, **2.** was taking, **3.** poured, **4.** had, **5.** were tagged, **6.** passed, **7.** were, **8.** had been refused, **9.** had, **10.** got, **11.** had been detained, **12.** were cared, **13.** kept, **14.** would decide, **15.** had passed, **16.** arrived, **17.** were, **18.** needed, **19.** became, **20.** got, **21.** were waiting

Unit 10 Shakespeare live (Key)

1 Vocabulary: Theatre life

1. to take, to create a role; **2.** to paint, to create a portrait; **3.** to make, to earn a living; **4.** to choose a topic; **5.** to direct, to publish, to write a play; **6.** to found a theatre; **7.** to watch a performance; **8.** to publish, to write, to choose a book; **9.** to join, to found, to choose an actors' company; **10.** to write, to publish, to choose a script; **11.** to raise, to earn, to make money; **12.** to create a character

2 Finding alternative expressions

1. to establish oneself, **2.** to deal with, **3.** to be at one's disposal, **4.** to dedicate to, **5.** to be associated with, **6.** to put a face to, **7.** to belong to, **8.** to earn a living, **9.** to be involved in, **10.** to be suspected of, **11.** to be based on

3 Life at the Globe Theatre

a)–b) Individuelle Schüler/innenantworten

4 Language in use: Celebrating Shakespeare's Birthday

0: time, **00:** ✓, **Q1:** of, **Q2:** well, **Q3:** ✓, **Q4:** ✓, **Q5:** time, **Q6:** ✓, **Q7:** song, **Q8:** skills, **Q9:** ✓, **Q10:** leisure, **Q11:** of, **Q12:** alive, **Q13:** horror, **Q14:** artist, **Q15:** ✓, **Q16:** never, **Q17:** ✓, **Q18:** certificate, **Q19:** ✓, **Q20:** money, **Q21:** favourite

5 Language in use: Sam Wanamaker – The man who revived the Globe Theatre

0: House, **00:** ✓, **Q1:** then, **Q2:** out, **Q3:** ✓, **Q4:** production, **Q5:** had, **Q6:** pockets, **Q7:** ✓, **Q8:** even

6 Language in use: Being a literary critic is not easy

0: C, **Q1:** B, **Q2:** C, **Q3:** D, **Q4:** A, **Q5:** D, **Q6:** B, **Q7:** B, **Q8:** C, **Q9:** B, **Q10:** D, **Q11:** A, **Q12:** A, **Q13:** D

Units 11–20 (Prime Time 8) Key

Unit 11 Ireland (Key)

1 Finding the right meaning

1. K, **2.** F, **3.** D, **4.** L, **5.** I, **6.** C, **7.** B, **8.** J, **9.** E, **10.** A, **11.** G, **12.** H

2 Language in use: Irish literature

0: small
Q1: books/works
Q2: ancient
Q3: ruled
Q4: differs
Q5: authors/writers
Q6: writer/author
Q7: important
Q8: tradition

3 Rephrasing: Events in Irish history

Beispielantwort

1. In the 12ᵗʰ century England first attacked/invaded Ulster, the northern part of the island, before it took full control in 1177.
2. In the 17ᵗʰ century the "Plantation of Ulster" was formed. English and Scottish settlers systematically colonised the northern part of the island. After the English Civil War the English forces under Oliver Cromwell occupied the whole of Ireland.
3. In 1690 the Protestant King William of Orange beat the ousted King James at the Battle of the Boyne and strengthened England's hold of Ireland.
4. In 1800 the Parliamentary Union of Ireland and Britain was formed.
5. In 1916 an uprising was staged against British rule, but it was suppressed and the Irish had to surrender. The leaders of the "Easter Rising" were sentenced to death and shot.

4 Plural forms

a) **-is → -es:** analyses, bases, crises, theses
 -o → -es: heroes , potatoes, tomatoes, volcanoes
 . . . → -es: boxes , bushes , classes , foxes, matches
 -f(e) → -ves: calves, halves, knives, leaves, lives, -selves, shelves, thieves, wolves
 -ey → -eys: journeys, keys
 -oo- → -ee-: feet, geese, teeth
 -on → -a: criteria, phenomena
 -um → -a: bacteria, curricula, media
 -ouse → -ice: lice, mice
 Complete change: children, men, oxen, women

No change (singular): craft, deer, fish, offspring, sheep, species
No change (plural): headquarters, means, series
b) Individuelle Schüler/innenantworten

5 Language in use: The Queen and the IRA commander

0: C, **Q1:** B, **Q2:** C, **Q3:** A, **Q4:** B, **Q5:** D, **Q6:** B, **Q7:** B, **Q8:** A, **Q9:** B, **Q10:** C, **Q11:** D, **Q12:** D

6 Language in use: Saint Patrick's Day

0: K, **Q1:** J, **Q2:** P, **Q3:** H, **Q4:** E, **Q5:** M, **Q6:** L, **Q7:** O, **Q8:** G, **Q9:** N, **Q10:** F, **Q11:** C, **Q12:** B, **Q13:** I; **Not used:** backpackers (A), converse (D)

Unit 12 Saving the planet (Key)

1 Climate change

a) 1. **biofuel:** fuel derived from renewable, biological sources including crops such as maize and sugar cane
 2. **carbon dioxide (CO_2):** principal greenhouse gas produced by human activity, by-product of human activities such as burning fossil fuels
 3. **carbon footprint:** amount of carbon emitted by an individual or organisation in a given period of time
 4. **climate change:** pattern of change affecting the global or regional climate such as average temperature and rainfall
 5. **deforestation:** permanent removal of standing forests leading to significant levels of carbon dioxide emissions
 6. **fossil fuels:** formed in the Earth over millions of years, produce carbon dioxide when burned
 7. **global warming:** steady rise in global average temperature largely caused by man-made greenhouse gas emissions
 8. **greenhouse effect:** insulating effect of certain gases in the atmosphere, allows solar radiation to warm the earth
 9. **mitigation:** action that will reduce man-made climate change by reducing greenhouse gas emissions or absorbing greenhouse gases in the atmosphere
 10. **renewable energy:** energy created from sources that can be replenished in a short period of time; biomass, the movement of water, geothermal, wind, and solar

11. **weather:** state of the atmosphere with regard to temperature, cloudiness, rainfall, wind and other meteorological conditions

b) **1.** biofuel, **2.** carbon footprint, **3.** greenhouse effect, **4.** deforestation, **5.** fossil fuels, **6.** Renewable energy, **7.** weather, **8.** mitigation

2 Language in use: Severn Suzuki's speech at the UN Earth Summit

a) **0:** A, **Q1:** A, **Q2:** C, **Q3:** B, **Q4:** C, **Q5:** D, **Q6:** D, **Q7:** B, **Q8:** C, **Q9:** D, **Q10:** A, **Q11:** A, **Q12:** D

b) Individuelle Schüler/innenantworten

3 Building a sustainable food source

1. is going to decrease, **2.** will have to, **3.** is going to stay, **4.** are going to see, **5.** isn't running out, **6.** will need, **7.** is getting, **8.** will be, **9.** will think, **10.** will be empowered, **11.** might become, **12.** is continuing, **13.** are going to have

4 "Passive houses" vs. "Active houses"

a) **1.** site, **2.** insulated, **3.** absorb, **4.** windows, **5.** loss, **6.** stale, **7.** moisture, **8.** low, **9.** expensive, **10.** climates

b)–c) Individuelle Schüler/innenantworten

Unit 13 Gender issues (Key)

1 Finding the right meaning

a) **1.** 18, **3.** 14, **5.** 22, **7.** 30, **9.** 16, **11.** 2, **13.** 26, **15.** 6, **17.** 10, **19.** 24, **21.** 28, **23.** 4, **25.** 12, **27.** 20, **29.** 8

b)–c) Individuelle Schüler/innenantworten

2 How to speculate

a) **1.** reflected on, **2.** review, **3.** read between the lines, **4.** guess, **5.** figure out, **6.** suspected, **7.** wondered

b) **1.** D, **2.** C, **3.** B, **4.** F, **5.** I, **6.** A, **7.** E, **8.** G, **9.** H

3 Language in use: I do not want to give up "me"

0: N, **Q1:** O, **Q2:** C, **Q3:** K, **Q4:** B, **Q5:** P, **Q6:** G, **Q7:** D, **Q8:** I, **Q9:** H, **Q10:** A, **Q11:** J, **Q12:** E, **Q13:** L;
Not used: consider (F), make up for (M)

4 Vocabulary: Living with children

a)–b) Individuelle Schüler/innenantworten

5 Are single women discriminated against at work?

Your co-worker with a three-year-old leaves at 5:30 every evening, while you stay until 7:30 (at least). You're asked to take a weekend shift or deal with Saturday conference calls because everyone else on your team has kids they need to spend time with. When an issue needs to be sorted out after six, you are somehow always the only one available, and it's made clear that your date plans are not a priority.

If this sounds like you, you may be the victim of what a recent *Marie Claire* article calls "the newest form of workplace discrimination: Single women who carry an unfair burden at the office, and stand in for their married-with-kids co-workers."

Employers have got used to working parents leaving at a reasonable hour and not working weekends, they've also got used to single staffers, particularly single women, picking up the work that employees with kids won't get to. The result for those single women is no personal life, which limits both their overall well-being and their ability to meet a prospective partner and have children of their own.

Even if single men face the same dilemma, it's easy to see how single women are especially vulnerable to it. The most popular job for American women as of 2010 is still secretary/administrative assistant, which has been a top ten job for women for the last 50 years. We're historically conditioned to think of female workers as those who support other workers. At the same time, women have just been told to be as ambitious as they can, which can very easily translate into saying "yes" to whatever project is handed to them.

6 Language in use: Female authors who use male pseudonyms

0: super, **00:** ✓, **Q1:** friend, **Q2:** of, **Q3:** over, **Q4:** ✓, **Q5:** in, **Q6:** modern, **Q7:** ✓, **Q8:** out, **Q9:** no, **Q10:** ✓, **Q11:** last, **Q12:** ✓, **Q13:** to, **Q14:** first, **Q15:** role, **Q16:** ✓, **Q17:** not, **Q18:** ✓, **Q19:** black

7 English similes

a) **1.** I, **2.** J, **3.** A, **4.** F, **5.** B, **6.** K, **7.** L, **8.** E, **9.** D, **10.** G, **11.** H, **12.** C

b) **1.** a lamb, **2.** gold, **3.** a wolf, **4.** life, **5.** the hills, **6.** a church mouse, **7.** a razor, **8.** a dog, **9.** silk, **10.** a ghost

c) as stubborn as a mule – as sturdy as an oak – as tall as a giraffe – as timid as a mouse – as wise as an owl – as white as snow – as tough as old boots – as quick as lightning – as silent as the grave – as slippery as an eel – as slow as a snail – as strong as an ox – as straight as an arrow – as solid as a rock

Unit 14 Migration (Key)

1 Analysing statistics

b) **1.** bar, **2.** number, **3.** refers, **4.** represented/depicted/shown, **5.** draw, **6.** see, **7.** peaked/rose, **8.** dropped,

9. decrease/decline, **10.** low, **11.** closely, **12.** notice/see/detect, **13.** permanent, **14.** surge/increase/rise

c) Individuelle Schüler/innenantworten

2 Word formation: The story of Filipino immigration to Canada

a)
- to achieve, achiever, achievement, achievable
- to arrive, arriver, arrival, arriving
- to connect, connector, connection/connective, connectable/connective
- to dedicate, dedicator, dedication, dedicated
- to elect, electee, election, electable
- to facilitate, facilitator, facilitation, facilitative
- –, –, immediacy, immediate
- to immigrate, immigrant, immigration, immigrating
- to integrate, –, integration, integrable
- to nurse, nurse, nursing, nursing
- –, –, permanency/permanence, permanent
- to reside, resident, residency, residing
- to settle, settler, settlement, settled
- to sponsor, sponsor, sponsorship, sponsored
- to strengthen, –, strengthening, strong

b) 1. strengthening, **2.** residency, **3.** nursed, **4.** arrival, **5.** connectable, **6.** immediate, **7.** dedication, **8.** election, **9.** permanent, **10.** achievable

c) 0: immigration
Q1: residents
Q2: arrivals/arrivers
Q3: immediate
Q4: permanent
Q5: achieved
Q6: sponsorship/sponsoring
Q7: settle
Q8: nursing
Q9: dedicated
Q10: facilitates
Q11: integrated
Q12: elected
Q13: strengthening
Q14: connection

3 Migrating to the United States

a) 1. parts, **2.** contributions, **3.** enrich, **4.** legacy, **5.** apply, **6.** loyalty, **7.** rewarded, **8.** privileges

b) 1. to qualify, **2.** permanent, continuous, **3.** eligible, **4.** criminal record, **5.** to deny, **6.** applicant, **7.** to declare, **8.** oath

4 Language in use: Why immigrants are more successful than you

a) 0: do, **00:** ✓, **Q1:** ✓, **Q2:** in, **Q3:** also, **Q4:** with, **Q5:** ✓, **Q6:** insurance, **Q7:** ✓, **Q8:** when, **Q9:** ✓, **Q10:** other, **Q11:** calling, **Q12:** experts, **Q13:** ✓, **Q14:** story, **Q15:** the, **Q16:** ✓, **Q17:** seen, **Q18:** ✓, **Q19:** almost, **Q20:** neither, **Q21:** ✓, **Q22:** so, **Q23:** why, **Q24:** what, **Q25:** ✓, **Q26:** you

b) Have you heard the saying that the grass is greener on the other side? For immigrants, it usually is greener. Although they may not be living in a fancy home or a rich neighbourhood when they first immigrate, those living conditions are still better than the ones they came from. This is why they rarely complain about life because there really is nothing to be sad about. In their eyes, life is truly good. They have a roof over their heads and their kids are getting a great education.

The next time you see an immigrant walking by, don't judge them because of their job, the way they talk or the clothes they wear. Be careful, as some of the richest immigrants I know still drive their beat-up car that is fifteen years old and they buy their clothes from Wal-Mart, and only when they are on sale.

Immigrants are successful because of their beliefs and the way they were brought up. So, take a page out of their book and learn a few things from them because it isn't too late for you to do so and, more importantly, to become successful.

Unit 15 One world (Key)

1 Word search

1. reconciliation, **2.** thrive, **3.** step in, **4.** stalemate, **5.** pursue, **6.** unprecedented, **7.** capacity, **8.** death toll, **9.** disarmament, **10.** devastating, **11.** proliferation, **12.** proactive, **13.** resolve problems, **14.** agenda, **15.** perception, **16.** invigorate, **17.** concerted, **18.** entail, **19.** transition, **20.** deploy

2 Word families

a) Beispielantwort
- to fail, failure, failure, failing, scheitern
- to prevent, –, prevention, preventable, verhindern
- to afford, –, affordability, affordable, ermöglichen
- to maintain, –, maintenance, maintained, aufrechterhalten
- to promote, promoter, promotion, –, fördern
- –, human (being), humanity, humanitarian, Mensch
- to ratify, –, ratification, ratified, ratifizieren
- –, –, permanence, permanent, Dauerhaftigkeit
- to interdepend, –, interdependence, interdependent, voneinander abhängen
- to endorse sth., –, endorsement, endorsed, beipflichten
- to deter sb., –, deterrent, deterring, jmd. abhalten
- to fluctuate, –, fluctuation, fluctuating, schwanken
- –, –, adequacy, adequate, Angemessenheit
- to annihilate, –, annihilation, annihilated, auslöschen

- to issue, issuer, issue, issued, ausstellen
- –, agent, agency, –, Ermittler
- to perform, performer, performance, performing, vorführen
- to oblige, –, obligation, obligatory, verpflichten
- to recommend, –, recommendation, recommendable, empfehlen

b)–c) Individuelle Schüler/innenantworten

3 Language in use: Médecins Sans Frontières wins Nobel Peace Prize

0: C, **Q1:** B, **Q2:** D, **Q3:** A, **Q4:** B, **Q5:** A, **Q6:** D, **Q7:** B, **Q8:** D, **Q9:** C, **Q10:** C, **Q11:** A, **Q12:** D

4 Criticism of the role of the UN in international conflicts

1. to prevent, **2.** to bring to mind, **3.** the original intent, **4.** most of humanity, **5.** ashes, **6.** body, **7.** partners, **8.** sound, **9.** to pick up, **10.** was bound to fail

5 Language in use: Oxfam – An international charity

0: ball, **00:** ✓, **Q1:** organisation, **Q2:** ✓, **Q3:** else, **Q4:** ✓, **Q5:** up, **Q6:** box, **Q7:** ✓, **Q8:** ✓, **Q9:** attack, **Q10:** engineering, **Q11:** less, **Q12:** up, **Q13:** ✓, **Q14:** the, **Q15:** ✓, **Q16:** workers, **Q17:** trap, **Q18:** ✓, **Q19:** ✓, **Q20:** not, **Q21:** more, **Q22:** ✓, **Q23:** ✓, **Q24:** outside

6 Synonyms

1. D, **2.** A, **3.** G, **4.** F, **5.** B, **6.** C, **7.** E

Unit 16 The individual and society (Key)

1 Maslow's hierarchy of needs

a) Beispielantwort
1. **Physiological needs:** air, food, shelter from the environment, sleep, water
2. **Safety needs:** healthcare, safe neighbourhood, security, steady employment
3. **Love needs:** acceptance, affection, belonging, companionship
4. **Esteem needs:** accomplishment, personal worth, social recognition
5. **Self-actualising needs:** fulfilling one's potential, personal growth

b) 1. hierarchy, **2.** motivated, **3.** basic, **4.** complex, **5.** accomplishment, **6.** affection, **7.** potential, **8.** shelter, **9.** recognition, **10.** steady

2 Volunteering

a) 1. organise the cleaning of the beaches
2. work with children to organise theatre plays
3. work with communities to resolve local clashes
4. teach basic life support skills in schools
5. be the front rider on a tandem bike so that blind people can enjoy cycling
6. help toads cross the road when they migrate for the breeding season

b) Individuelle Schüler/innenantworten
c) 1. giving up, **2.** learning difficulties, **3.** Olympic Games, **4.** free time, **5.** selfish, **6.** life partner, **7.** love lives, **8.** speed-dating, **9.** fitness, **10.** lost weight

3 Language in use: Personal freedom

0: J, **Q1:** H, **Q2:** I, **Q3:** A, **Q4:** L, **Q5:** B, **Q6:** F, **Q7:** C, **Q8:** E, **Q9:** K; **Not used:** emotional (D), obvious (G)

4 The American Dream

a) Beispielantwort
Category 1: Verb
to be blessed with sth., to pass a law, to pursue a dream, to roll up your sleeves
Category 2: Adjective
persistent, powerful, proud
Category 3: Noun
baby-boomer, civil rights, country of boundless possibilities, distance, equality of opportunity, fortune, freedom, gender equality, glory, heritage, liberty, minority group, nation, patriotism, poverty, rags-to-riches, road to success, social climbing, Stars and Stripes, success, tolerance, wealth

b) Individuelle Schüler/innenantworten
c) In den Originalzitaten fehlende Ausdrücke:
1. persistent, **2.** proud, **3.** roll up your sleeves, **4.** distance, **5.** road to success, **6.** success
Sprachlich auch richtig:
1. powerful, **2.** powerful, **3.** pursue a dream, **4.** –, **5.** country of boundless possibilities, **6.** fortune/ freedom/glory/liberty/wealth

5 Expressing yourself in the right register

a) Informal register: 1. to blow sb. off, **2.** to pick sb.'s brains, **3.** to chow down sth., **4.** goombah, **5.** to cabbage sth.
Formal register: 1. to disregard sb. on purpose, **2.** to require to know, **3.** to take nourishment, **4.** confidant, **5.** to take sth. without permission
b) Individuelle Schüler/innenantworten

Unit 17 Big money (Key)

1 Proverbs and sayings

1. G, **2.** E, **3.** F, **4.** A, **5.** C, **6.** H, **7.** D, **8.** B

2 Language in use: Compulsive shopping

0: the, **00:** ✓, **Q1:** us, **Q2:** mall, **Q3:** ✓, **Q4:** good, **Q5:** idea, **Q6:** only, **Q7:** fantasy, **Q8:** room, **Q9:** the, **Q10:** ✓, **Q11:** ✓, **Q12:** not, **Q13:** ✓, **Q14:** yourself, **Q15:** out, **Q16:** ✓

3 Word families

a) Individuelle Schüler/innenantworten
b) Beispielantwort
  to respond: responsible, responsibility, irresponsible, irresponsibility, responder, responsive, irresponsive
  to add: addition, additional, additionally, additive
  to defend: defender, defensive, defence, defendant, defending
  to judge: judgement, judgemental, misjudge, misjudgement

4 Language in use: Daniel Kahneman on income

0: Education
Q1: inequality
Q2: determine
Q3: satisfaction
Q4: difference(s)
Q5: happiness
Q6: inevitably
Q7: unhappy
Q8: experiencing
Q9: disability
Q10: resident
Q11: distinctive/distinguishing
Q12: greatly
Q13: depending
Q14: continued/continuous/continuing
Q15: significant

5 Language in use: Using social media for marketing

0: C, **Q1:** B, **Q2:** C, **Q3:** B, **Q4:** A, **Q5:** D, **Q6:** A, **Q7:** B, **Q8:** B, **Q9:** D, **Q10:** A, **Q11:** D, **Q12:** B

6 Language in use: Consumerism among children

a) **0:** N, **Q1:** C, **Q2:** J, **Q3:** G, **Q4:** L, **Q5:** M, **Q6:** B, **Q7:** A, **Q8:** H, **Q9:** O, **Q10:** E, **Q11:** P, **Q12:** I, **Q13:** D;
  Not used: busy (F), negotiation (K)
b) **1.** there is no doubt, **2.** to persuade, **3.** aspect, **4.** TV advert, **5.** consumer, **6.** brand, **7.** strategies

Unit 18 Science and technology (Key)

1 Surveillance and the media

a) Beispielantwort
  1. Their job was to analyse data on suspicious activity on government servers.
  2. India denies having carried out a domestic surveillance programme on electronic communication.
  3. We strongly suspect that the government has collected information on the internet activities of our company.
  4. Several EU states are believed to have intercepted encrypted messages on social networking websites.
  5. The new law has sparked a general debate on the surveillance of citizens.
  6. The US has tightened the security on transatlantic flights, which has caused several complaints about unreasonable searches.
b) **1.** obtained, **2.** records, **3.** details, **4.** subscriber, **5.** promotes, **6.** accused, **7.** addresses, **8.** publish, **9.** uncomfortable, **10.** articulating, **11.** boundaries, **12.** invasion
c) Individuelle Schüler/innenantworten

2 Language in use: How big brother spies on pupils

0: A, **Q1:** B, **Q2:** A, **Q3:** C, **Q4:** B, **Q5:** D, **Q6:** D, **Q7:** A, **Q8:** A, **Q9:** C, **Q10:** C

3 Genetic engineering

a) **1.** announced, **2.** sperm, **3.** conception, **4.** couples, **5.** share, **6.** described, **7.** latest, **8.** processes, **9.** undertaken, **10.** infertile
b) **0:** of, **00:** ✓, **Q1:** been, **Q2:** ✓, **Q3:** certificate, **Q4:** ✓, **Q5:** time, **Q6:** ✓, **Q7:** ✓, **Q8:** inside, **Q9:** although, **Q10:** across, **Q11:** before, **Q12:** ✓, **Q13:** not, **Q14:** also, **Q15:** out, **Q16:** ✓, **Q17:** her, **Q18:** ✓, **Q19:** not, **Q20:** a, **Q21:** nevertheless, **Q22:** moreover, **Q23:** shelters, **Q24:** ✓

4 Foods with benefits

a) Beispielantwort
Start in Aisle 2: Here is grape juice <u>for your heart</u>. In Aisle 5: <u>Vitamin-packed</u> water for <u>your immune system</u>. In aisle after aisle, wonders beckon. Foods and drinks to <u>help your heart</u>, <u>lower your cholesterol</u>, <u>trim your tummy</u>. Toss them into your cart and you might feel better. You might even live longer.

  Or not. Because this, shoppers, is the question: Are all these products really <u>healthy</u>, or are some of them just <u>hyped</u>? Over the past decade, functional food has turned into a big business. And more Americans are buying into the functional story. But as sales soar, federal regulators worry that some <u>packaged foods that scream healthy</u> on their labels <u>are in fact no healthier than</u> many ordinary brands. They have been cracking down on products that, in their view, <u>make dubious claims</u> and <u>bamboozle shoppers with slick marketing</u>.

No one is saying that these products are <u>unsafe</u> or <u>unhealthy</u>, or that there isn't science behind them. But nutritionists say that the vast number of functional foods <u>has left many consumers</u> confused about the products' actual health value. And, in some cases, manufacturers are bending or even breaking the rules about how they market these products. Companies promote myriad processed foods that have been <u>loaded with vitamins and nutrients</u>, or <u>contain a potentially beneficial ingredient</u>, as wellness aids. For many, these <u>"healthified" foods</u> have become the new health food. Many Americans are willing to pay a premium for <u>ready-to-heat and on-the-go foods</u> that seem to promise shortcuts to healthier living.

However, the bureau of consumer protection is concerned that people who buy foods that, for instance, <u>claim to bolster immunity</u> or <u>reduce the risk of prostate cancer</u> might forgo a flu shot or a doctor's visit.

The situation is clearer in Europe, where authorities have set up an independent panel of experts to check every health claim. Food makers submit applications with scientific evidence for a specific claim. The panel then reviews each case and issues an opinion on whether the evidence shows that eating the food indeed causes the advertised effect. A list of approved health claims is intended to make food shopping less confusing – at least for consumers in Europe.

b) **Beispielantwort**
Positive: Vitamin-packed, loaded with vitamins and nutrients, contain a potentially beneficial ingredient
Neutral: for your heart, for your immune system, help your heart, lower your cholesterol, trim your tummy, healthy, unsafe, unhealthy, has left many consumers confused, ready-to-heat and on-the-go foods, claim to bolster immunity, reduce the risk of prostate cancer
Negative: hyped, packaged foods that scream healthy, are in fact no healthier than, make dubious claims, bamboozle shoppers with slick marketing, "healthified" foods

c) **1.** vitamin-packed, **2.** to beckon, **3.** to turn into sth., **4.** to buy into sth., **5.** to crack down on sth., **6.** to bamboozle sb., **7.** myriad, **8.** healthified, **9.** ready-to-heat, **10.** to forgo sth.

5 The language of science: Location-based apps and the future of shopping

a) **Beispielantwort**
It is a current trend that more and more smartphone apps **require access** to location data **provided by** the phone's built-in GPS module. According to a 2012 report, three-quarters of America's smartphone owners use their devices to **retrieve information** related to their location. Such location data is promising to advertisers. They can begin sending customers so-called hyperlocal advertising, tailored not just to the city, but to a particular city block.

The technology **is called** "geofencing", which has been used for years in the ankle bracelets worn by accused criminals under constant surveillance. A judge might grant a criminal suspect permission to go to her job, her church and her local supermarket, with each approved location plugged into the court's computer system. Data from the ankle-strapped GPS could confirm that the suspect was staying out of mischief or send a warning to police when she went to a prohibited location.

Geofencing also has other uses, for example for parents who want to know about their children's whereabouts. The service **retrieves location data** from a child's phone and sends a message whenever the child arrives at home or at school or leaves again.

When marketers build a geofence, they have no desire to restrict customers' movements. The goal is to detect people's close approach to a nearby business that is looking to make a sale, so the company can ping customers with a text message urging them to buy. Because marketers realise that nobody wants a constant stream of text messages, a policy of "frequency capping" is practiced. Customers generally get no more than five messages a week, even if many other attractive deals come within range.

Still, geofencing **is rarely used by** advertisers nowadays. The technology **requires constantly recalculating** the phone's position, which shortens battery life quickly. Yet, even if geofencing becomes more energy efficient, it might still not be **a sound strategy** for selling many consumer products.

As psychologists found out, valuable things are usually not consumed spontaneously. It is highly unlikely that a customer, alerted by his phone that a half-price sale on expensive consumer technology is taking place in a store nearby, will act upon sudden impulse and seriously consider the offer. Even at the lower price, such items will cost hundreds of dollars

_and are thus the sort of purchase consumers think about and plan for.

b) **Beispielantwort**

Present tense, passive constructions

c) **1.** location data, **2.** retrieve information, **3.** geofencing, **4.** constant surveillance, **5.** sound strategy, **6.** upon sudden impulse

Unit 19 Ideals and reality (Key)

1 Synonyms

1. G, **2.** O, **3.** J, **4.** L, **5.** H, **6.** M, **7.** P, **8.** N, **9.** B, **10.** D, **11.** F, **12.** K, 13. I, 14. E, 15. C, 16. A

2 Finding opposites

active – passive; aggressive – defensive; biased – fair; formal – informal; funny, humorous – serious, sincere; matter-of-fact – ironic, sarcastic

3 Language in use: Modern slavery

0: C, **Q1:** B, **Q2:** C, **Q3:** B, **Q4:** D, **Q5:** A, **Q6:** D, **Q7:** B, **Q8:** C, **Q9:** A, **Q10:** A, **Q11:** C

4 Language in use: HIV/AIDS in Hollywood movies

a) **0:** F, **Q1:** A, **Q2:** C, **Q3:** E, **Q4:** J, **Q5:** K, **Q6:** N, **Q7:** O, **Q8:** L, **Q9:** M, **Q10:** G, **Q11:** B, **Q12:** D, **Q13:** I; **Not used:** losing (H), written (P)

b) **1.** ways of thinking, **2.** to allow us, **3.** medications, **4.** to be limited to, **5.** to plague, **6.** stigma

5 Tesla's next move

0: humming
Q1: robotic
Q2: assembly
Q3: Farther/Further
Q4: environmentally
Q5: Specifically
Q6: competitive
Q7: helping
Q8: enduring
Q9: prevailing
Q10: affordable
Q11: performance
Q12: calculation
Q13: brilliance
Q14: pollution

6 What is political correctness?

0: pattern, **00:** ✓, **Q1:** way, **Q2:** new, **Q3:** ✓, **Q4:** useful, **Q5:** only, **Q6:** ✓, **Q7:** ✓, **Q8:** hardly, **Q9:** out, **Q10:** ✓, **Q11:** ✓, **Q12:** themselves, **Q13:** not, **Q14:** ✓, **Q15:** away, **Q16:** not, **Q17:** ✓, **Q18:** ✓, **Q19:** never, **Q20:** ✓, **Q21:** ✓, **Q22:** level

7 Paraphrasing

Beispielantwort

1. According to the survey the people in Europe are aware of the consequences of climate change.
2. Many people think that politicians should do more to reduce carbon dioxide emissions quickly.
3. The number of people who think climate change is a serious problem has risen in the last two years.
4. Political leaders should not underestimate the problem because that would be even worse.

Unit 20 Lifelong learning (Key)

1 Expressing an opinion

a) **1.** know, **2.** unlearn, **3.** love, **4.** preparation, **5.** follow, **6.** stays young, **7.** graduates, **8.** imitation, **9.** taught

b) Individuelle Schüler/innenantworten

2 Home schooling: If a child gets bored at school, blame the system

a) Individuelle Schüler/innenantworten

b) **1.** curious, **2.** eagerness, **3.** fascination, **4.** frustration, **5.** idling, **6.** novelty, **7.** repetitive, **8.** stimulating

c) **0:** questions
Q1: heading/going
Q2: course
Q3: coin
Q4: looking
Q5: decided
Q6: curriculum
Q7: week
Q8: off
Q9: after
Q10: answer

d) **1.** F, **2.** G, **3.** H, **4.** E, **5.** B, **6.** C, **7.** D, **8.** A

3 Taking a gap year

a) Individuelle Schüler/innenantworten

b) **1.** academic year, **2.** finishing school, **3.** encourage, **4.** pick up, **5.** degree course, **6.** voluntary work, **7.** looking for adventure, **8.** see more of the world, **9.** save up, **10.** gap packages

c) Individuelle Schüler/innenantworten

4 Language in use: Applying for university

a) **0:** rate, **00:** of, **Q1:** ✓, **Q2:** both, **Q3:** ✓, **Q4:** Although, **Q5:** after, **Q6:** ✓, **Q7:** ✓, **Q8:** ceremonies, **Q9:** book, **Q10:** the, **Q11:** ✓, **Q12:** being, **Q13:** ✓, **Q14:** will, **Q15:** not, **Q16:** neither, **Q17:** trip, **Q18:** ✓, **Q19:** ✓, **Q20:** complaint, **Q21:** ✓

b) 1. express my interest in, **2.** will be graduating, **3.** solid intellectual foundation, **4.** academic achievement, **5.** transferable skills, **6.** highly motivated, **7.** application form

Sample Matura tasks **Key**

1   Multiple choice: Migrants in Mexico waiting to cross

0: C, **Q1:** B, **Q2:** C, **Q3:** C, **Q4:** A, **Q5:** D, **Q6:** B, **Q7:** C, **Q8:** C, **Q9:** B

2   Banked gap fill: Sport paves the way

0: E, **Q1:** K, **Q2:** L, **Q3:** G, **Q4:** J, **Q5:** H, **Q6:** D, **Q7:** I, **Q8:** F, **Q9:** N, **Q10:** R, **Q11:** O, **Q12:** A, **Q13:** C, **Q14:** P, **Q15:** B; **Not used:** realised (M), tendency (Q)

3   Open gap fill: Paper cups

0: new
Q1: fast food/coffee
Q2: popular/common/widespread
Q3: concerns/reasons/regulations/considerations
Q4: used
Q5: replaced
Q6: designed/made/intended
Q7: end
Q8: substances/materials

4   Editing: Gennaro Contaldo – Jamie Oliver's mentor

0: dress, **00:** ✓, **Q1:** along, **Q2:** ✓, **Q3:** under, **Q4:** the, **Q5:** often, **Q6:** ✓, **Q7:** his, **Q8:** ✓, **Q9:** the, **Q10:** ✓, **Q11:** were, **Q12:** of, **Q13:** only, **Q14:** ✓

5   Word formation: Alcoholics Anonymous

0: organisation
Q1: illness
Q2: entrance
Q3: regulations
Q4: political
Q5: frustration(s)
Q6: pressure
Q7: suffering
Q8: abuse
Q9: addicted
Q10: uneasy
Q11: indications/indicators
Q12: closer

6   Multiple choice: Is queuing really the British way?

0: C, **Q1:** D, **Q2:** D, **Q3:** C, **Q4:** B, **Q5:** B, **Q6:** A, **Q7:** A, **Q8:** C, **Q9:** A

7   Banked gap fill: What's proper social media etiquette at a celebrity wedding?

0: L, **Q1:** C, **Q2:** H, **Q3:** G, **Q4:** F, **Q5:** K, **Q6:** D, **Q7:** J, **Q8:** B, **Q9:** E; **Not used:** affront (A), secret (I)

8   Open gap fill: Project helps parents to help their children

0: made
Q1: ago
Q2: educational
Q3: without
Q4: many
Q5: subjects
Q6: from
Q7: even
Q8: taking
Q9: take
Q10: how

9   Editing: As lovely as a tree? Poem in UK cleanses air pollution

0: like, **00:** ✓, **Q1:** neither, **Q2:** in, **Q3:** insurance, **Q4:** an, **Q5:** ✓, **Q6:** other, **Q7:** one, **Q8:** ✓, **Q9:** ✓, **Q10:** masks, **Q11:** not, **Q12:** ✓, **Q13:** across, **Q14:** ✓, **Q15:** store, **Q16:** by, **Q17:** about, **Q18:** ✓, **Q19:** whether, **Q20:** behind, **Q21:** ✓

10   Word formation: Does folk art include your nan's knitting?

0: sized
Q1: conceptual
Q2: exhibition
Q3: products
Q4: industrial(ised)
Q5: definitions
Q6: labelled
Q7: arrived
Q8: choosing
Q9: declaring
Q10: admitted
Q11: investigation
Q12: Alternatively

Bildquellen:

U1 FusionPix (Corbis); **5.1** Akabei (Thinkstock); **5.2** julien Tromeur (iStockphoto.com); **6** stevanovicigor (Thinkstock); **7** L-house (Thinkstock); **9** M.studio (Fotolia.com); **10** urfinguss (Thinkstock); **11** nightman1965 (Thinkstock); **12** Sebastian Kaulitzki (iStockphoto.com); **13** KatarzynaBialasiewicz (Thinkstock); **14.1–5** vector1st (Thinkstock); **16** IPGGutenbergUKLtd (Thinkstock); **17** Sharron_Miller (Thinkstock); **19.1** Georg Hellmayr; **19.2** Wong Sze Fei (Fotolia. com); **20** shvili (Thinkstock); **21** alexsokolov (Thinkstock); **22.1** Mallivan (Thinkstock); **22.2** Björn Meyer (iStockphoto. com); **24.1–3** Pia Moest (öbv); **25** PIKSEL (Thinkstock); **26** miracky (Thinkstock); **28** Chris Johnson (Thinkstock); **29.1** Georg Hellmayr; **29.2** Nastia11 (Thinkstock); **30** kailash soni (Thinkstock); **31** Creatas (Thinkstock); **32** Pete Klinger 2009 (Thinkstock); **33** Creatas (Thinkstock); **34** sundikova (Thinkstock); **37** cybrain (Thinkstock); **38** IPGGutenbergUKLtd (Thinkstock); **39.1** halbergman (iStockphoto.com); **39.2** Jan Rose (Fotolia.com); **39.3** Sergey Nivens (Thinkstock); **39.4** Purestock (Thinkstock); **39.5** korionov (Thinkstock); **39.6** Baran Özdemir (iStockphoto.com); **40** Wavebreakmedia Ltd. (Thinkstock); **42.1–6** tony4urban (Thinkstock); **44** Dario Lo Presti (Thinkstock); **45** RomoloTavani (Thinkstock); **47** Nikhil Gangavane (iStockphoto.com); **48** nimu1956 (iStockphoto.com); **49.1** Georg Hellmayr; **49.2** Vasiliki Varvaki (iStockphoto.com); **49.3** Alexandr Tkachuk (iStockphoto.com); **49.4** Marcin Chodorowski (Fotolia.com); **49.5** Digitalpress (Fotolia.com); **49.6** zhudifeng (iStockphoto.com); **50.1, 3, 5, 7, 9** Smileus (Fotolia.com); **50.2, 4, 6, 8, 10** t.light (iStockphoto.com); **51** Georg Hellmayr; **55** MEV-Verlag, Germany; **58** Spike Mafford (Thinkstock); **60** Fuse (Thinkstock); **62** Wolfgang Jargstorff (Fotolia.com); **63** violetkaipa (Thinkstock); **65.1–15** MH Foto Design; **66** MEV-Verlag, Germany; **69** Stephan Waba; **70** Believe_In_Me (Thinkstock); **71** Arthur Carlo Franco (Thinkstock); **72** max_776 (Fotolia.com); **74** Pia Moest (öbv); **76** Stockbyte (Thinkstock); **77** stevanovicigor (Thinkstock); **79** Yuri Arcurs (Fotolia.com); **80** michaeljung (Thinkstock); **81** joggiebotma (Thinkstock); **82** Laura Flugga (Thinkstock); **83** Carol Thacker (Thinkstock); **84.1–9** asafta (Thinkstock); **86** Matton Images; **91** IPGGutenbergUKLtd (Thinkstock); **92** truembie (Thinkstock); **93** LDProd (Thinkstock); **94** Vladimir Nenov (Thinkstock); **96** Elena Schweitzer (Fotolia.com); **97** Anthony Brown (Thinkstock); **100** wanderluster (Thinkstock); **102** Don Bayley (Thinkstock); **104** simeyla (Thinkstock); **105** Ingram Publishing (Thinkstock); **107** WW5 (Thinkstock); **109** picsfive (Fotolia.com); **110** VRD (Fotolia.com); **111** RalfenByte (Fotolia.com); **112** PeJo (Fotolia.com)

Textquellen:

6 www.worldaffairsjournal.org; **7** www.telegraph.co.uk; **8** www.independent.co.uk; **16** www.brighthubeducation.com; **17** www.travelandleisure.com; **18** flavorwire.com; **20** www.wikihow.com; **25** newyork.cbslocal.com; **26** www.newyorker.com; **38** www.rollingstone.com; **44** racerelations.about.com; **47** www.bbc.co.uk; **57** www.dailymail.co.uk; **58** www.history.com; **62** metro.co.uk; **66** www.theguardian.com; **67** www.huffingtonpost.com; **71** www.cicnews.com; **73** www.quicksprout.com; **76** www.theguardian.com; **77** communities.washingtontimes.com; **81** www.telegraph.co.uk; **83** www.theguardian.com; **86** edge.org; **87** www.wordstream.com; **90** www.theguardian.com; **92** www.nytimes.com; **93** blogs.discovermagazine.com; **96** news.thestigmaproject.org; **97** www.slate.com; **100** www.telegraph.co.uk; **104** www.economist.com; **108** www.bbc.com; **109** news.instyle.com; **110** www.southwalesargus.co.uk; **111** www.techtimes.com; **112** www.theguardian.com